HANS CHRISTIAN ANDERSEN
BY HIMSELF

HANS CHRISTIAN ANDERSEN
From a Photograph of 1870

Hans Christian Andersen

THE TRUE STORY OF MY LIFE
BY
Hans Christian Andersen

ISBN: 1-58963-465-9

Copyright © 2001 by Fredonia Books

Reprinted from the 1926 edition

Fredonia Books
Amsterdam, The Netherlands

Fredonia Books
Amsterdam, The Netherlands

Hans Christian Andersen:
The True Story of My Life

by
Hans Christian Andersen

ISBN: 1-58963-465-9

Reprinted from the 1926 edition

Fredonia Books
Amsterdam, The Netherlands
http://www.fredoniabooks.com

TO

JENNY LIND

THE

ENGLISH TRANSLATION

OF

THE TRUE STORY OF HER FRIEND'S LIFE

IS INSCRIBED

IN ADMIRATION OF HER BEAUTIFUL TALENTS

AND STILL MORE BEAUTIFUL LIFE

BY

MARY HOWITT

PREFACE

WHEN ANDERSEN wrote the story of his life, here printed in its original form, he had reached the height of international fame. He was surrounded by kind friends, welcomed by kings and princes, courted by poets and scholars. The struggles of his youth were behind him, but he had not travelled so far away from them that he had lost the warm glow of satisfaction in difficulties overcome. The shadows of old age were still distant. He had found the true medium of his genius in the fairy tales, and he was yet in the fullness of his creative power.

It was natural, therefore, that he should look back upon his life as " a lovely story, happy and full of incident ", and that he should think it could not have been happier or better even if a kind fairy had given the poor, friendless boy the power to choose his own career. The sufferings of the boy and youth had sunk into the background of his consciousness, and yet we need only listen to the undertones of his story to feel how poignant they had been, and how they had influenced the whole bent of his mind.

From other sources we have a somewhat darker picture of his home and family than that which he has drawn for us with such idyllic charm. There was an inherited strain of insanity and moral weakness. Even his parents were failures from the viewpoint of model citizenship, but they seem to have given him a heritage of temperament and warmth of heart. He loved his mother deeply, grieved over her death, and raised a protecting hand over her memory in the story "*Good-for-Nothing*". From his father, who took him walking, told him folk stories, and read Holberg and Arabian Nights to him, he seems to have received impulses that afterwards blossomed in his fairy tales.

Hans Christian's conviction that he was destined for a great actor or a great poet brought upon the awkward, ignorant lad ridicule from which he suffered intensely. No doubt these early humiliations together with his sense of dependence had the effect of making him all his life inordinately sensitive to every pin-prick of criticism. On the other hand, he expanded like a flower in the sun to every smile of encouragement. With the soul-searching that was habitual to him, he often asked himself: "Is this vanity?" but answered his own question by saying that praise made him humble.

When he records the homage done him in Sweden he adds that it " scorched the roots of pride rather than nourished them ".

It was his affection rather than his vanity which was wounded when his kind friends, the Collin family, refused to take him seriously. When he came home from abroad and told of the friendship shown him by the Duke of Saxe-Weimar, old Fru Collin looked at him dubiously, and asked, " Are you sure they were not making fun of you, Andersen ? " His gratitude to the Collins has been officially, and most sincerely, recorded in his autobiography. The unofficial story of his relations with them is written in *The Ugly Duckling*. The Conference Councillor himself is the old woman whose house was a haven of refuge and who was reputed to know more than any one else in the world. The younger generation of Collins have been perpetuated in the cat and the hen who tried so energetically to model Ugly Duckling Andersen in their own correct and efficient image.

Andersen never married and never had a home of his own. During a large part of his life he regarded the Collin household as his real home. In his old age he was equally domesticated in the home of a cultured Jewish family, Melchior by name, and it was in their country house, Rolighed, that he died. in 1875.

Hans Christian Andersen's autobiography, *Mit Livs Eventyr*, is here published in the form in which he originally wrote it for the German edition of his works, in 1846. The translation by Mary Howitt, the pioneer English translator from Scandinavian literature, from whose hand we have also Fredrika Bremer's works, appeared shortly afterwards under the title *The True Story of My Life*. Andersen twice added to this book, not only bringing it up to date, but also expanding and altering the earlier chapters. Many of these additions, while interesting in themselves, deal with people and events unfamiliar to American readers and they break the continuity of the story. The Committee on Publications has therefore thought it best to use the earlier edition, which retains the freshness and naïve simplicity of an Andersen fairy tale. We are fortunate, too, in having this edition in the version of Mary Howitt, whose delicately precise English has the flavor of Andersen's own leisurely age.

HANNA ASTRUP LARSEN.

CONTENTS

HANS CHRISTIAN ANDERSEN

THE TRUE STORY OF MY LIFE

CHAPTER I

My life is a lovely story, happy and full of incident. If, when I was a boy, and went forth into the world poor and friendless, a good fairy had met me and said, " Choose now thy own course through life, and the object for which thou wilt strive, and then, according to the development of thy mind, and as reason requires, I will guide and defend thee to its attainment." my fate could not, even then, have been directed more happily, more prudently, or better. The history of my life will say to the world what it says to me—There is a loving God, who directs all things for the best.

My native land, Denmark, is a poetical land, full of popular traditions, old songs, and an eventful history, which has become bound up with that of Sweden and Norway. The Danish islands are possessed of beautiful beech woods, and corn and clover fields : they resemble gardens on a great scale. Upon one of these green islands, Funen, stands Odense, the place of my birth. Odense is called after the pagan god Odin, who, as tradition states, lived here : this place is the capital of the province, and lies twenty-two Danish miles from Copenhagen.

In the year 1805 there lived here, in a small mean room, a young married couple, who were extremely attached to each other: he was a shoe-maker, scarcely twenty two years old, a man of a richly gifted and truly poetical mind. His wife, a few years older than himself, was ignorant of life and of the world, but possessed a heart full of love. The young man had himself made his shoemaking bench, and the bedstead with which he began housekeeping ; this bedstead he had made out of the wooden frame which had borne only a short time before the coffin of the deceased Count Trampe, as he lay in state, and the remnants of the black cloth on the wood work kept the fact still in remembrance.

Instead of a noble corpse, surrounded by crape and wax-lights, here lay, on the second of April 1805, a living and weeping child,—that was my-self, Hans Christian Andersen. During the first day of my existence my father is said to have sate by the bed and read aloud in Holberg, but I cried all the time. " Wilt thou go to sleep, or listen quietly?" it is reported that my father asked in joke; but I still cried on; and even in the church, when I was taken to be baptized, I cried so loudly that the preacher, who was a passionate man, said, " The young one screams like a cat! " which words my mother never forgot. A poor emigrant Gomar, who stood as godfather, consoled her in the mean time by saying that the louder I cried as a child, all the more beautifully should I sing when I grew older.

Our little room, which was almost filled with the shoemaker's bench, the bed, and my crib, was the abode of my childhood; the walls, however, were covered with pictures, and over the work-bench was a cupboard containing books and songs; the little kitchen was full of shining plates and metal pans, and by means of a ladder it was possible to go out on the roof, where, in the gutters between our and the neighbour's house, there stood a great chest filled with soil, my mother's sole garden, and where she grew her vegetables. In my story of the Snow Queen that garden still blooms.

I was the only child, and was extremely spoiled, but I continually heard from my mother how very much happier I was than she had been, and that I was brought up like a nobleman's child. She, as a child, had been driven out by her parents to beg, and once when she was not able to do it, she had sate for a whole day under a bridge and wept. I have drawn her character in two different aspects, in old Dominica, in the Improvisatore, and in the Mother of Christian, in Only a Fiddler.

My father gratified me in all my wishes. I possessed his whole heart; he lived for me. On Sundays he made me perspective glasses, theatres, and pictures which could be changed; he read to me from Holberg's plays and the Arabian Tales; it was only in such moments as these that I can remember to have seen him really cheerful, for he never felt himself happy in his life and as a handicrafts-man. His parents had been country people in good circumstances, but upon whom many misfortunes had fallen: the cattle had died; the farm house had been burned down; and lastly, the husband had lost his reason. On this the wife had removed with him to Odense, and there put her son, whose mind was full of intelligence, apprentice to a shoemaker; it could not be otherwise, although it was his ardent wish to be able to attend the Grammar School, where he might have learned Latin. A few well-to-do citizens had at one time spoken of this, of clubbing together a sufficient sum to pay for his board and education, and thus giving him a start in life; but it never went beyond words. My poor father saw his dearest wish unfulfilled; and he never lost the remembrance of it. I recollect that once, as a child, I saw tears in his eyes, and it was when a youth from the Grammar School came to our house to be measured for a new pair of boots, and showed us his books and told us what he learned.

"That was the path upon which I ought to have gone!" said my father, kissed me passionately, and was silent the whole evening.

He very seldom associated with his equals. He went out into the woods on Sundays, when he took me with him; he did not talk much when he was out, but would sit silently, sunk in deep thought, whilst I ran about and strung strawberries on a bent, or bound garlands. Only twice in the year, and that in the month of May, when the woods were arrayed in their earliest green, did my mother go with us, and then she wore a cotton gown, which she put on only on these occasions, and when she partook of the Lord's Supper, and which, as long as I can remember, was her holiday gown. She always took home with her from the wood a great many fresh beech boughs, which were then planted behind the polished stone. Later in the year sprigs of St. John's Wort were stuck into the chinks of the beams, and we considered their growth as omens whether our lives would be long or short. Green branches and pictures ornamented our little room, which my mother always kept neat and clean; she took great pride in always having the bed-linen and the curtains very white.

The mother of my father came daily to our house, were it only for a moment, in order to see her little grandson. I was her joy and her delight. She was a quiet and most amiable old woman, with mild blue eyes and a fine figure, which life had severely tried. From having been the wife of a countryman in easy circumstances she had now fallen into great poverty, and dwelt with her feeble-minded husband in a little house, which was the last, poor remains of their property. I never saw her shed a tear; but it made all the deeper impression upon me when she quietly sighed, and told me about her own mother's mother, how she had been a rich noble lady, in the city of Cassel, and that she had married a "comedy-player," that was as she expressed it, and run away from parents and home, for all of which her posterity had now to do penance. I never can recollect that I heard her mention the family name of her grandmother; but her own maiden name was Nommesen. She was employed to take care of the gardens belonging to a lunatic asylum, and every Sunday evening she brought us some flowers, which they gave her permission to take home with her. These flowers adorned my mother's cupboard; but still they were mine, and to me it was allowed to put them in the glass of water. How great was this pleasure! She brought them all to me; she loved me with her whole soul. I knew it, and I understood it.

She burned, twice in the year, the green rubbish of the garden; on such occasions she took me with her to the asylum, and I lay upon the great heaps of green leaves and pea-straw. I had many flowers to play with, and—which was a circumstance upon which I set great importance—I had here better food to eat than I could expect at home.

All such patients as were harmless were permitted to go freely about the court; they often came to us in the garden, and with curiosity and terror I listened to them and followed them about; nay, I even ventured so far as to go with the attendants to those who were raving mad. A long passage led to their cells. On one occasion, when the attendants were out of the way, I lay down upon the floor, and peeped through the crack of the door into one of these cells. I saw within a lady almost naked, lying on her straw bed; her hair hung down over her shoulders, and she sang with a very beautiful voice. All at once she sprang up, and threw herself against the door where I lay; the little valve through which she received her food burst open; she stared down upon me, and stretched out her long arm towards me. I screamed for terror—I felt the tips of her fingers touching my clothes—I was half dead when the attendant came; and even in later years that sight and that feeling remained within my soul.

Close beside the place where the leaves were

burned the poor old women had their spinning room. I often went in there, and was very soon a favourite. When with these people, I found myself possessed of an eloquence which filled them with astonishment. I had accidentally heard about the internal mechanism of the human frame, of course without understanding anything about it; but all these mysteries were very captivating to me; and with chalk, therefore, I drew a quantity of flourishes on the door, which were to represent the intestines; and my description of the heart and the lungs made the deepest impression. I passed for a remarkably wise child, that would not live long; and they rewarded my eloquence by telling me tales in return; and thus a world as rich as that of the thousand and one nights was revealed to me. The stories told by these old ladies, and the insane figures which I saw around me in the asylum, operated in the meantime so powerfully upon me, that when it grew dark I scarcely dared go out of the house. I was therefore permitted, generally at sunset, to lay me down in my parent's bed with its long flowered curtains, because the press-bed in which I slept could not conveniently be put down so early in the evening on account of the room it occupied in our small dwelling; and here, in the paternal bed, lay I in a waking dream, as if the actual world did not concern me.

I was very much afraid of my weak-minded grandfather. Only once had he ever spoken to me, and then he had made use of the formal pronoun, "you." He employed himself in cutting out of wood strange figures, men with beasts heads and beasts with wings; these he packed in a basket and carried them out into the country, where he was everywhere well received by the peasant women, because he gave to them and their children these strange toys. One day, when he was returning to Odense, I heard the boys in the street shouting after him; I hid myself behind a flight of steps in terror, for I knew that I was of his flesh and blood.

Every circumstance around me tended to excite my imagination. Odense itself, in those days in which there was not a single steamboat in existence, and when intercourse with other places was much more rare than now, was a totally different city to what it is in our day; a person might have fancied himself living hundreds of years ago, because so many customs prevailed then which belonged to an earlier age. The guilds walked in procession through the town with their harlequin before them with mace and bells; on Shrove Tuesday the butchers led the fattest ox through the streets adorned with garlands, whilst a boy in a white shirt and with great wings on his shoulders rode upon it ; the sailors paraded through the city with music and all their flags flying and then two of the boldest among them stood and wrestled upon a plank placed between two boats, and the one who was not thrown into the water was the victor.

That, however, which more particularly stamped itself upon my memory, and became refreshed by after often-repeated relations, was, the abode of the Spaniards in Funen in 1808. It is true that at that time I was but three years old; still I nevertheless perfectly remember the brown foreign men who made disturbance in the streets, and the cannon which were fired. I saw the people lying on straw in a half-tumble down church, which was near the asylum. One day, a Spanish soldier took me in his arms and pressed a silver image, which he wore upon his breast, to my lips. I remember that my mother was angry at it, because, she said, there was something papistical about it; but the image, and the strange man, who danced me about, kissed me and wept, pleased me: certainly he had children at home in Spain. I saw one of his comrades led to execution; he had killed a Frenchman. Many years afterwards this little circumstance occasioned me to write my little poem, "The Soldier," which Chamisso translated into German, and which afterwards was included in the illustrated people's books of soldier-songs.*

I very seldom played with other boys; even at school I took little interest in their games, but remained sitting within doors. At home I had playthings enough, which my father made for me. My greatest delight was in making clothes for my dolls, or in stretching out one of my mother's aprons between the wall and two sticks before a currant-bush which I had planted in the yard, and thus to gaze in between the sun-illumined leaves. I was a singularly dreamy child, and so constantly went about with my eyes shut, as at last to give the impression of having weak sight, although the sense of sight was especially cultivated by me.

Sometimes, during the harvest, my mother went

* This same little song, sent to me by the author, was translated by me and published in the 19th No. of Howitt's Journal.—M.H.

into the field to glean. I accompanied her, and
we went, like Ruth in the Bible, to glean in the
rich fields of Boaz. One day we went to a place
the bailiff of which was well known for being a
man of rude and savage disposition. We saw him
coming with a huge whip in his hand, and my
mother and all the others ran away. I had wooden
shoes on my bare feet, and in my haste I lost these,
and then the thorns pricked me so that I could
not run, and thus I was left behind and alone.
The man came up and lifted his whip to strike
me, when I looked him in the face and involuntarily exclaimed,—

"How dare you strike me, when God can see
it?"

The strong, stern man looked at me, and at
once became mild; he patted me on the cheeks,
asked me my name, and gave me money.

When I brought this to my mother and showed
it her, she said to the others, "He is a strange
child, my Hans Christian; everybody is kind to
him: this bad fellow even has given him money."

I grew up pious and superstitious. I had no
idea of want or need; to be sure my parents had
only sufficient to live from day to day, but I at

least had plenty of every thing; an old woman altered my father's clothes for me. Now and then I went with my parents to the theatre, where the first representations which I saw were in German. " *Das Donauweibchen* " was the favourite piece of the whole city; there, however, I saw, for the first time, Holberg's Village Politicians treated as an opera.

The first impression which a theatre and the crowd assembled there made upon me was, at all events, no sign of anything poetical slumbering in me; for my first exclamation on seeing so many people was, " Now, if we only had as many casks of butter as there are people here, then I would eat lots of butter!" The theatre, however, soon became my favourite place, but, as I could only very seldom go there, I acquired the friendship of the man who carried out the play-bills, and he gave me one every day. With this I seated myself in a corner and imagined an entire play, according to the name of the piece and the characters in it. That was my first, unconscious poetising.

My father's favourite reading was plays and stories, although he also read works of history and the scriptures. He pondered in silent thought afterwards upon that which he had read, but my mother did not understand him when he talked with her about it, and therefore he grew more and more silent. One day he closed the Bible with the words, "Christ was a man like us, but an extraordinary man!" These words horrified my mother, and she burst into tears. In my distress I prayed to God that he would forgive this fearful blasphemy in my father. "There is no other devil than that which we have in our own hearts," I heard my father say one day, and I made myself miserable about him and his soul; I was therefore entirely of the opinion of my mother and the neighbours, when my father, one morning, found three scratches on his arm, probably occasioned by a nail, that the devil had been to visit him in the night, in order to prove to him that he really existed.

My father's rambles in the wood became more frequent; he had no rest. The events of the war in Germany, which he read in the newspapers with eager curiosity, occupied him completely. Napoleon was his hero: his rise from obscurity was the most beautiful example to him. At that time Denmark was in league with France; nothing was

talked of but war; my father entered the service as
a soldier, in the hope of returning home a lieu-
tenant. My mother wept, the neighbours shrug-
ged their shoulders, and said that it was folly to
go out to be shot when there was no occasion for it.

The morning on which the corps were to march
I heard my father singing and talking merrily,
but his heart was deeply agitated; I observed that
by the passionate manner in which he kissed me
when he took his leave. I lay sick of the measles
and alone in the room, when the drums beat, and
my mother accompanied my father, weeping, to
the city gate. As soon as they were gone my old
grandmother came in; she looked at me with her
mild eyes and said, it would be a good thing if I
died; but that God's will was always the best.

That was the first day of real sorrow which I
remember.

The regiment advanced no farther than Holstein, peace was concluded, and the voluntary
soldier returned to his work-stool. Every thing
fell into its old course. I played again with my
dolls, acted comedies, and always in German,
because I had only seen them in this language;
but my German was a sort of gibberish which I

A Corner in Old Odense near the Andersen Home
In the Background St. Knud's Church

made up, and in which there occurred only one real German word, and that was "*Besen*," a word which I had picked up out of the various dialects which my father brought home from Holstein.

"Thou hast indeed some benefit from my travels," said he in joke. God knows whether thou wilt get as far; but that must be thy care. Think about it, Hans Christian!" But it was my mother's intention that, as long as she had any voice in the matter, I should remain at home, and not lose my health as he had done.

That was the case with him: his health had suffered. One morning he woke in a state of the wildest excitement, and talked only of campaigns and Napoleon. He fancied that he had received orders from him to take the command. My mother immediately sent me, not to the physician, but to a so-called wise woman some miles from Odense. I went to her. She questioned me, measured my arm with a woollen thread, made extraordinary signs, and at last laid a green twig upon my breast. It was, she said, a piece of the same kind of tree upon which the Saviour was crucified.

"Go now," said she, "by the river side

towards home. If your father will die this time, then you will meet his ghost."

My anxiety and distress may be imagined,— I, who was so full of superstition, and whose imagination was so easily excited.

"And thou hast not met any thing, hast thou?" inquired my mother when I got home. I assured her, with beating heart, that I had not.

My father died the third day after that. His corpse lay on the bed; I therefore slept with my my mother. A cricket chirped the whole night through.

"He is dead," said my mother, addressing it; "thou needest not call him. The ice maiden has fetched him."

I understood what she meant. I recollected that, in the winter before, when our window panes were frozen, my father pointed to them and showed us a figure as that of a maiden with outstretched arms. "She is come to fetch me," he said, in jest. And now, when he lay dead on the bed, my mother remembered this, and it occupied my thoughts also.

He was buried in St. Knud's Churchyard, by the door on the left-hand side coming from the altar. My grandmother planted roses upon his grave. There are now in the self-same place two strangers' graves, and the grass grows green upon them also.

After my father's death, I was entirely left to myself. My mother went out washing. I sate alone at home with my little theatre, made doll's clothes, and read plays. It has been told me that I was always clean and nicely dressed. I had grown tall; my hair was long, bright, and almost yellow, and I always went bare-headed. There dwelt in our neighbourhood the widow of a clergyman, Madame Bunkeflod, with the sister of her deceased husband. This lady opened to me her door, and hers was the first house belonging to the educated class into which I was kindly received. The deceased clergyman had written poems, and had gained a reputation in Danish literature. His spinning songs were at that time in the mouths of the people. In my vignettes to the Danish poets I thus sang of him whom my contemporaries had forgotten :—

> Spindles rattle, wheels turn round,
>   Spinning-songs depart ;
> Songs which youth sings soon become
>   Music of the heart.

Here it was that I heard for the first time the word *poet* spoken, and that with so much reverence, as proved it to be something sacred. It is true that my father had read Holberg's plays to me; but here it was not of these that they spoke, but of verses and poetry. " My brother the poet," said Bunkeflod's sister, and her eyes sparkled as she said it. From her I learned that it was a something glorious, a something fortunate, to be a poet. Here, too, for the first time, I read Shakspeare, in a bad translation, to be sure; but the bold descriptions, the heroic incidents, witches, and ghosts were exactly to my taste. I immediately acted Shakspeare's plays on my little puppet theatre. I saw Hamlet's ghost, and lived upon the heath with Lear. The more persons died in a play, the more interesting I thought it. At this time I wrote my first piece: it was nothing less than a tragedy, wherein, as a matter of course, every body died. The subject of it I borrowed from an old song about Pyramus and Thisbe; but I had increased the incidents through a hermit and his son, who both loved Thisbe, and who both killed themselves when she died. Many speeches of the hermit were passages from the Bible, taken out of the little catechism, especially from our duty to our neighbours. To the piece I gave the title " Abor and Elvira."

"It ought to be called ' Perch (Aborre) and Stockfish,' " said one of our neighbours wittily to me as I came with it to her after having read it with great satisfaction and joy to all the people in our street. This entirely depressed me, because I felt that she was turning both me and my poem to ridicule. With a troubled heart, I told it to my mother.

"She only said so," replied my mother, " because her son had not done it." I was comforted, and began a new piece, in which a king and queen were among the dramatis personæ. I thought that it was not quite right that these dignified personages, as in Shakspeare, should speak like other men and women. I asked my mother and different people how a king ought properly to speak, but no one knew exactly. They said that it was so many years since a king had been in Odense, but that he certainly spoke in a foreign language. I procured myself, therefore, a sort of lexicon, in which were German, French, and English words with Danish meanings, and this helped me. I took a word out of each language, and inserted them into the speeches of my king and queen, It was a regular Babel-like language, which I considered only suitable for such elevated personages.

I desired now that every body should hear my piece. It was a real felicity to me to read it aloud, and it never occurred to me that others should not have the same pleasure in listening to it.

The son of one of our neighbours worked in a cloth manufactory, and every week brought home a sum of money. I was at a loose end, people said, and got nothing. I was also now to go to the manufactory, " not for the sake of the money," my mother said, " but that she might know where I was, and what I was doing."

My old grandmother took me to the place, therefore, and was very much affected, because, said she, she had not expected to live to see the time when I should consort with the poor ragged lads that worked there.

Many of the journeymen who were employed in the manufactory were Germans; they sang and were merry fellows, and many a coarse joke of theirs filled the place with loud laughter. I heard them, and I there learned that, to the innocent ears of a child, the impure remains very unintelligible. It took no hold upon my heart. I was possessed at that time of a remarkably beautiful and high soprano voice, and I knew it; because when I sang in my parents' little garden, the people in the street stood and listened, and the fine folks in the garden of the states-councillor, which adjoined ours, listened at the fence. When, therefore, the people at the manufactory asked me whether I could sing, I immediately began, and all the looms stood still: all the journeymen listened to me. I had to sing again and again, whilst the other boys had my work given to them to do. I now told them that I also could act plays, and that I knew whole scenes of Holberg and Shakspeare. Every body liked me; and in this way the first days in the manufactory passed on very merrily. One day, however, when I was in my best singing vein, and every body spoke of the extraordinary brilliancy of my voice, one of the journeymen said that I was a girl, and not a boy. He seized hold of me. I cried and screamed. The other journeymen thought it very amusing, and held me fast by my arms and legs. I screamed aloud, and was as much ashamed as a girl; and then, darting from them, rushed home to my mother, who immediately promised me that I should never go there again.

I again visited Madame Bunkeflod, for whose birthday I invented and made a white silk pincushion. I also made an acquaintance with another old clergyman's widow in the neighbourhood. She permitted me to read aloud to her the works which she had from the circulating library. One of them began with these words:— "It was a tempestuous night; the rain beat against the window-panes."

" That is an extraordinary book," said the old lady; and I quite innocently asked her how she knew that it was. "I can tell from the beginning," said she, "that it will turn out extraordinary."

I regarded her penetration with a sort of reverence.

Once in the harvest time my mother took me with her many miles from Odense to a nobleman's seat in the neighbourhood of Bogense, her native place. The lady who lived there, and with whose parents my mother had lived, had

said that some time she might come and see her
That was a great journey for me: we went most
of the way on foot, and required, I believe, two
days for the journey. The country here made
such a strong impression upon me, that my most
earnest wish was to remain in it, and become a
countryman. It was just in the hop-picking
season; my mother and I sat in the barn with a
great many country people round a great binn,
and helped to pick the hops. They told tales as
they sat at their work, and every one related what
wonderful things he had seen or experienced.
One afternoon I heard an old man among them
say that God knew every thing, both what had
happened and what would happen. That idea
occupied my whole mind, and towards evening,
as I went alone from the court, where there was
a deep pond, and stood upon some stones which
were just within the water, the thought passed
through my head, whether God actually knew
every thing which was to happen there. Yes, he
has now determined that I should live and be so
many years old, thought I; but, if I now were to
jump into the water here and drown myself, then
it would not be as he wished; and all at once I was

firmly and resolutely determined to drown myself. I ran to where the water was deepest, and then a new thought passed through my soul. " It is the devil who wishes to have power over me!" I uttered a loud cry, and, running away from the place as if I were pursued, fell weeping into my mother's arms. But neither she nor any one else could wring from me what was amiss with me.

"He has certainly seen a ghost," said one of the women; and I almost believed so myself.

My mother married a second time, a young handicraftsman; but his family, who also belonged to the handicraft class, thought that he had married below himself, and neither my mother nor myself were permitted to visit them. My step-father was a young, grave man, who would have nothing to do with my education. I spent my time, therefore, over my peep-show and my puppet theatre, and my greatest happiness consisted in collecting bright coloured pieces of cloth and silk, which I cut out myself, and sewed. My mother regarded it as good exercise preparatory to my becoming a tailor, and took up the idea that I certainly was born for it. I, on the contrary, said that I would go to the theatre and be an actor, a wish which my mother most sedulously opposed, because she knew of no other theatre than those of the strolling players and the rope-dancers. No, a tailor I must and should be. The only thing which in some measure reconciled me to this prospect was, that I should then get so many fragments to make up for my theatre.

My passion for reading, the many dramatic scenes which I knew by heart, and my remarkably fine voice, had turned upon me in some sort the attention of several of the more influential families of Odense. I was sent for to their houses, and the peculiar characteristics of my mind excited their interest. Among others who noticed me was the Colonel Hoegh-Guldberg, who with his family showed me the kindest sympathy; so much so, indeed, that he introduced me to the present king, then Prince Christian.

I grew rapidly, and was a tall lad, of whom my mother said that she could not let him any longer go about without any object in life. I was sent, therefore, to the charity school, but learned only religion, writing, and arithmetic, and the last badly enough; I could also scarcely spell a word correctly. On the master's birthday I always wove him a garland and wrote him a poem; he received them half with smiles and half as a joke: the last time, however, he scolded me. The street lads had also heard from their parents of my peculiar turn of mind, and that I was in the habit of going to the houses of the gentry. I was therefore one day pursued by a wild crowd of them, who shouted after me derisively, " There runs the play-writer !" I hid myself at home in a corner, wept, and prayed to God.

My mother said that I must be confirmed, in order that I might be apprenticed to the tailor trade, and thus do something rational. She loved me with her whole heart, but she did not understand my impulses and my endeavours, nor indeed at that time did I myself. The people about her always spoke against my odd ways, and turned me to ridicule.

We belonged to the parish of St. Knud, and the candidates for confirmation could either enter their names with the provost or the chaplain. The children of the so-called superior families and the scholars of the grammar school went to the first, and the children of the poor to the second. I however, announced myself as a candidate to the provost, who was obliged to receive me, although he discovered vanity in my placing myself among his catechists, where, although taking the lowest place, I was still above those who were under the care of the chaplain. I would, however, hope that it was not alone vanity which impelled me. I had a sort of fear of the poor boys, who had laughed at me, and I always felt as it were an inward drawing towards the scholars of the grammar school, whom I regarded as far better than other boys. When I saw them playing in the church-yard, I would stand outside the railings, and wish that I were but among the fortunate ones,—not for the sake of play, but for the sake of the many books they had, and for what they might be able to become in the world. With the provost, there-fore, I should be able to associate with them, and be as they were; but I do not remember a single one of them now, so little intercourse would they hold with me. I had daily the feeling of having thrust myself in where people thought that I did not belong. One young girl, however, there was, and one who was considered too of the highest rank, whom I shall afterwards have to mention; she always looked gently and kindly at me, and even once gave me a rose. I returned home full of happiness, because there was one being who did not overlook and repel me.

An old female tailor altered my deceased father's great coat into a confirmation suit for me; never before had I worn so good a coat. I had also for the first time in my life a pair of boots. My delight was extremely great; my only fear was that every body would not see them, and therefore I drew them up over my trousers, and thus marched through the church. The boots creaked, and that inwardly pleased me, for thus the congregation would hear that they were new. My whole devotion was disturbed; I was aware of it, and it caused me a horrible pang of conscience that my thoughts should be as much with my new boots as with God. I prayed him earnestly from my heart to forgive me, and then again I thought about my new boots.

During the last year I had saved together a little sum of money. When I counted it over I found it to be thirteen rix dollars banco (about thirty shillings). I was quite overjoyed at the possession of so much wealth, and as my mother now most resolutely required that I should be

apprenticed to a tailor, I prayed and besought her
that I might make a journey to Copenhagen, that
I might see the greatest city in the world.

"What wilt thou do there?" asked my mother.

"I will become famous," returned I, and I
then told her all that I had read about extraordinary men. "People have," said I, "at first
an immense deal of adversity to go through, and
then they will be famous."

It was a wholly unintelligible impulse that
guided me. I wept, I prayed, and at last my
mother consented, after having first sent for a
so-called wise woman out of the hospital, that
she might read my future fortune by the coffee-
grounds and cards.

"Your son will become a great man," said the
old woman, "and in honour of him, Odense will
one day be illuminated."

My mother wept when she heard that, and I
obtained permission to travel. All the neighbours told my mother that it was a dreadful
thing to let me, at only fourteen years of age, go
to Copenhagen, which was such a long way off,
and such a great and intricate city, and where I
knew nobody.

" Yes," replied my mother, "but he lets me have no peace; I have therefore given my consent, but I am sure that he will go no further than Nyborg; when he gets sight of the rough sea, he will be frightened and turn back again."

During the summer before my confirmation, a part of the singers and performers of the Theatre Royal had been in Odense, and had given a series of operas and tragedies there. The whole city was taken with them. I, who was on good terms with the man who delivered the play-bills, saw the performances behind the scenes, and had even acted a part as page, shepherd, etc., and had spoken a few words. My zeal was so great on such occasions, that I stood there fully apparelled when the actors arrived to dress. By these means their attention was turned to me; my childlike manners and my enthusiasm amused them; they talked kindly with me, and I looked up to them as to earthly divinities. Every thing which I had formerly heard about my musical voice, and my recitation of poetry, became intelligible to me. It was the theatre for which I was born; it was there that I should become a famous man, and for that reason Copenhagen was the goal of my endeavours. I heard a deal said about the large theatre in Copenhagen, and that there was to be seen what was called the ballet, something which surpassed both the opera and the play: more especially did I hear the solo-dancer, Madame Schall, spoken of as the first of all. She therefore appeared to me as the queen of every thing, and in my imagination I regarded her as the one who would be able to do every thing for me, if I could only obtain her support. Filled with these thoughts, I went to the old printer Iversen, one of the most respectable citizens of Odense, and who, as I heard, had had considerable intercourse with the actors when they were in the town. He, I thought, must of necessity be acquainted with the famous dancer; him I would request to give me a letter of introduction to her, and then I would commit the rest to God.

The old man saw me for the first time, and heard my petition with much kindness; but he dissuaded me most earnestly from it, and said that I might learn a trade.

" That would actually be a great sin," returned I.

He was startled at the manner in which I said

that, and it prepossessed him in my favour; he confessed that he was not personally acquainted with the dancer, but still that he would give me a letter to her. I received one from him, and now believed the goal to be nearly won.

My mother packed up my clothes in a small bundle, and made a bargain with the driver of a post carriage to take me back with him to Copenhagen for three rix dollars banco. The afternoon on which we were to set out came, and my mother accompanied me to the city gate. Here stood my old grandmother; in the last few years her beautiful hair had become grey; she fell upon my neck and wept, without being able to speak a word. I was myself deeply affected. And thus we parted. I saw her no more; she died in the following year. I do not even know her grave: she sleeps in the poorhouse burial-ground.

The postilion blew his horn; it was a glorious sunny afternoon, and the sunshine soon entered into my gay child-like mind. I delighted in every novel object which met my eye, and I was journeying towards the goal of my soul's desires. When, however, I arrived at Nyborg on the great Belt, and was borne in the ship away from my native island, I then truly felt how alone and forlorn I was, and that I had no one else except God in heaven to depend upon.

As soon as I set foot on Zealand, I stepped behind a shed which stood on the shore, and falling on my knees, besought of God to help and guide me aright; I felt myself comforted by so doing, and I firmly trusted in God and my own good fortune. The whole day and the following night I travelled through cities and villages; I stood solitarily by the carriage, and ate my bread while it was repacked.—I thought I was far away in the wide world.

CHAPTER II

On Monday morning, September 5th, 1819, I saw from the heights of Fredricksberg, Copenhagen, for the first time. At this place I alighted from the carriage, and with my little bundle in my hand, entered the city through the castle garden, the long alley, and the suburb.

The evening before my arrival had been made memorable by the breaking out of the so-called Jews quarrel, which spread through many European countries. The whole city was in commotion* ; every body was in the streets; the noise and tumult of Copenhagen far exceeded, therefore, any idea which my imagination had formed of this, at that time, to me great city.

With scarcely ten dollars in my pocket, I turned into a small public-house. My first ramble was to the theatre. I went round it many times: I

---

* This remarkable disturbance makes a fine incident in Andersen's romance of "Only a Fiddler."—M. H.

looked up to its walls, and regarded them almost as a home. One of the-ticket sellers, who wandered about here each day, observed me, and asked me if I would have a ticket. I was so wholly ignorant of the world, that I thought the man wished to give me one; I therefore accepted his offer with thankfulness. He fancied I was making fun of him, and was angry ; so that I was frightened, and hastened from the place which was to me the dearest in the city. Little did I then imagine that ten years afterwards my first dramatic piece would be represented there, and that in this manner I should make my appearance before the Danish public.

On the following day I dressed myself in my confirmation suit, nor were the boots forgotten, although, this time, they were worn, naturally, under my trousers ; and thus, in my best attire, with a hat on, which fell half over my eyes, I hastened to present my letter of introduction to the dancer, Madame Schall. Before I rung at the bell, I fell on my knees before the door and prayed God that I here might find help and support. A maid-servant came down the steps with her basket in her hand ; she smiled kindly at me, gave me a skilling (Danish), and tripped on. Astonished, I looked at her and the money. I had on my confirmation suit, and thought I must look very smart. How then could she think that I wanted to beg? I called after her.

"Keep it, keep it!" said she to me, in return, and was gone.

At length I was admitted to the dancer; she looked at me in great amazement, and then heard what I had to say. She had not the slightest knowledge of him from whom the letter came, and my whole appearance and behaviour seemed very strange to her. I confessed to her my heartfelt inclination for the theatre; and upon her asking me what characters I thought I could represent, I replied Cinderella. This piece had been performed in Odense by the royal company, and the principal characters had so greatly taken my fancy, that I could play the part perfectly from memory. In the meantime I asked her permission to take off my boots, otherwise I was not light enough for this character; and then taking up my broad hat for a tambourine, I began to dance and sing:—

> "Here below, nor rank nor riches
> Are exempt from pain and woe."

My strange gestures and my great activity caused the lady to think me out of my mind, and she lost no time in getting rid of me.

From her I went to the manager of the theatre, to ask for an engagement. He looked at me, and said that I was " too thin for the theatre."

" Oh," replied I, " if you will only engage me with one hundred rix dollars banco salary, then I shall soon get fat !" The manager bade me gravely go my way, adding, that they only engaged people of education.

I stood there deeply wounded. I knew no one in all Copenhagen who could give me either counsel or consolation. I thought of death as being the only thing, and the best thing for me ; but even then my thoughts rose upwards to God, and with all the undoubting confidence of a child in his father, they riveted themselves upon Him. I wept bitterly, and then I said to myself, " When every thing happens really miserably, then he sends help. I have always read so. People must first of all suffer a great deal before they can bring any thing to accomplishment."

I now went and bought myself a gallery ticket for the Opera of Paul and Virginia. The separation of the lovers affected me to such a degree, that I burst into violent weeping. A few women, who sate near me, consoled me by saying that it was only a play, and nothing to trouble oneself about; and then they gave me a sausage sandwich. I had the greatest confidence in every body, and therefore I told them, with the utmost openness, that I did not really weep about Paul and Virginia, but because I regarded the theatre as my Virginia, and that if I must be separated from it, I should be just as wretched as Paul. They looked at me, and seemed not to understand my meaning. I then told them why I had come to Copenhagen, and how forlorn I was there. One of the women, therefore, gave me more bread and butter, with fruit and cakes.

On the following morning I paid my bill, and to my infinite trouble I saw that my whole wealth consisted in one rix dollar banco. It was necessary therefore, either that I should find some vessel to take me home, or put myself to work with some handicraftsman. I considered that the last was the wiser of the two, because, if I returned to Odense, I must there also put myself to work of a similar kind; besides which, I knew very well that the people there would laugh at me if I came back again. It was to me a matter of indifference what handicraft trade I learned,—I only should make use of it to keep life within me in Copenhagen. I bought a newspaper, therefore, and found among the advertisements that a cabinet maker was in want of an apprentice. The man received me kindly, but said that before I was bound to him he must have an attestation, and my baptismal register from Odense; and that till these came I could remove to his house, and try how the business pleased me. At six o'clock the next morning I went to the workshop: several journeymen were there, and two or three apprentices; but the master was not come. They fell into merry and idle discourse. I was as bashful as a girl, and as they soon perceived this, I was unmercifully rallied upon it. Later in the day the rude jests of the young fellows went so far, that, in remembrance of the scene at the manufactory, I took the resolute determination not to remain a single day longer in the workshop. I went down to the master, therefore, and told him that I could not stand it; he tried to console me, but in vain: I was too much affected, and hastened away.

I now went through the streets; nobody knew me; I was quite forlorn. I then bethought myself of having read in a newspaper in Odense the name of an Italian, Siboni, who was the director of the Academy of Music in Copenhagen. Every body had praised my voice; perhaps he would assist me for its sake; if not, then that very evening I must seek out the master of some vessel who would take me home again. At the thoughts of the journey home I became still more violently excited, and in this state of suffering I hastened to Siboni's house.

It happened that very day that he had a large party to dinner; our celebrated composer Weyse was there, the poet Baggesen, and other guests. The housekeeper opened the door to me, and to her I not only related my wish to be engaged as a singer, but also the whole history of my life. She listened to me with the greatest sympathy, and then she left me. I waited a long time, and she must have been repeating to the company the greater part of what I had said, for, in a while, the door opened, and all the guests came out and looked at me. They would have me to sing, and Siboni heard me attentively. I gave some scenes out of Holberg, and repeated a few poems; and then, all

at once, the sense of my unhappy condition so
overcame me that I burst into tears; the whole
company applauded.

" I prophesy," said Baggesen, " that one day
something will come out of him; but do not be
vain when, some day, the whole public shall
applaud thee!" and then he added something about
pure, true nature, and that this is too often destroyed by years and by intercourse with mankind.
I did not understand it all.

Siboni promised to cultivate my voice, and that
I therefore should succeed as a singer at the
Theatre Royal. It made me very happy; I
laughed and wept; and as the housekeeper led me
out and saw the excitement under which I laboured
she stroked my cheeks, and said that on the following day I should go to Professor Weyse, who
meant to do something for me, and upon whom I
could depend.

I went to Weyse, who himself had risen from
poverty; he had deeply felt and fully comprehended my unhappy situation, and had raised by
a subscription seventy rix dollars banco for me.
I then wrote my first letter to my mother, a letter
full of rejoicing, for the good fortune of the whole

world seemed poured upon me. My mother in her joy showed my letter to all her friends; many heard of it with astonishment; others laughed at it, for what was to be the end of it? In order to understand Siboni it was necessary for me to learn something of German. A woman of Copenhagen, with whom I travelled from Odense to this city, and who gladly, according to her means, would have supported me, obtained, through one of her acquaintances a language-master, who gratuitously gave me some German lessons, and thus I learned a few phrases in that language. Siboni received me into his house, and gave me food and instruction; but half a year afterwards my voice broke, or was injured, in consequence of my being compelled to wear bad shoes through the winter, and having besides no warm under-clothing. There was no longer any prospect that I should become a fine singer. Siboni told me that candidly, and counselled me to go to Odense, and there learn a trade.

I, who in the rich colours of fancy had described to my mother the happiness which I actually felt, must now return home and become an object of derision! Agonised with this thought, I stood as if crushed to the earth. Yet, precisely amid this apparently great unhappiness lay the stepping-stones of a better fortune.

As I found myself again abandoned, and was pondering by myself upon what was best for me next to do, it occurred to me that the Poet Guldberg, a brother of the Colonel of that name in Odense, who had shown me so much kindness, lived in Copenhagen. He lived at that time near the new church-yard outside the city, of which he has so beautifully sung in his poems. I wrote to him, and related to him everything; afterwards I went to him myself, and found him surrounded with books and tobacco pipes. The strong, warm-hearted man received me kindly; and as he saw by my letter how incorrectly I wrote, he promised to give me instruction in the Danish tongue; he examined me a little in German, and thought that it would be well if he could improve me in this respect also. More than this, he made me a pres-ent of the profits of a little work which he had just then published; it became known, and I believe they exceeded one hundred rix dollars banco; the excellent Weyse and others also supported me.

It was too expensive for me to lodge at a public

house; I was therefore obliged to seek for private lodgings. My ignorance of the world led me to a widow who lived in one of the most disreputable streets of Copenhagen; she was inclined to receive me into her house, and I never suspected what kind of a world it was which moved around me. She was a stern, but active dame; she described to me the other people of the city in such horrible colours as made me suppose that I was in the only safe haven there. I was to pay twenty rix dollars monthly for one room, which was nothing but an empty store-room, without window and light, but I had permission to sit in her parlour. I was to make trial of it at first for two days, meantime on the following day, she told me that I could decide to stay or immediately go. I, who so readily attach myself to people, already liked her, and felt myself at home with her, but more than sixteen dollars per month Weyse had told me I must not pay, and this was the sum which I had received from him and Guldberg, so that no surplus remained to me for my other expenses. This troubled me very much; when she was gone out of the room, I seated myself on the sofa, and contemplated the portrait of her deceased husband.

I was so wholly a child, that as the tears rolled down my own cheeks I wetted the eyes of the portrait with my tears, in order that the dead man might feel how troubled I was, and influence the heart of his wife. She must have seen that nothing more was to be drained out of me, for when she returned to the room she said that she would receive me into her house for the sixteen rix dollars. I thanked God and the dead man.

I found myself in the midst of the mysteries of Copenhagen, but I did not understand how to interpret them. There was in the house in which I lived a friendly young lady, who lived alone, and often wept; every evening her old father came and paid her a visit. I opened the door to him frequently; he wore a plain sort of coat, had his throat very much tied up, and his hat pulled over his eyes. He always drank his tea with her, and nobody dared to be present, because he was not fond of company: she never seemed very glad at his coming.* Many years afterwards, when I had reached another step on the ladder of life, when the refined world of fashionable life was opened before me, I saw one evening, in the midst of a brilliantly

* This character will be recognised in Steffen Margaret, in "Only a Fiddler."—M. H.

lighted hall, a polite old gentleman covered with orders—that was the old father in the shabby coat, he whom I had let in. He had little idea that I had opened the door to him when he played his part as guest, but I, on my side, then had also no thought but for my own comedy-playing; that is to say, I was at that time so much of a child that I played with my puppet-theatre and made my dolls' clothes; and in order that I might obtain gaily coloured fragments for this purpose, I used to go to the shops and ask for patterns of different kinds of stuffs and ribbons. I myself did not possess a single farthing; my landlady received all the money each month in advance; only now and then, when I did any errands for her, she gave me something, and that went in the purchase of paper and old play-books. I was now very happy, and was doubly so because Professor Guldberg had induced Lindgreen, the first comic actor at the theatre, to give me instruction. He gave me several parts in Holberg to learn, such as Hendrik, and the Silly Boy, for which I had shown some talent. My desire, however, was to play the Correggio. I obtained permission to learn this piece in my own way, although Lindgreen asked, with comic gravity, whether I expected to resemble the great painter? I, however, repeated to him the soliloquy in the picture gallery with so much feeling, that the old man clapped me on the shoulder and said, "Feeling you have; but you must not be an actor, though God knows what else. Speak to Guldberg about your learning Latin: that always opens the way for a student."

I a student! That was a thought which had never come before into my head. The theatre lay nearer to me, and was dearer too; but Latin I had also always wished to learn. But before I spoke on the subject to Guldberg, I mentioned it to the lady who gave me gratuitous instruction in German; but she told me that Latin was the most expensive language in the world, and that it was not possible to gain free instruction in it. Guldberg, however, managed it so that one of his friends, out of kindness, gave me two lessons a week.

The dancer, Dahlen, whose wife at that time was one of the first artistes on the Danish boards, opened his house to me. I passed many an evening there, and the gentle, warm-hearted lady was kind to me. The husband took me with him to

the dancing-school, and that was to me one step
nearer to the theatre. There stood I for whole
mornings, with a long staff, and stretched my
legs; but notwithstanding all my good-will, it was
Dahlen's opinion that I should never get beyond
a figurante. One advantage, however, I had
gained; I might in an evening make my appearance
behind the scenes of the theatre; nay, even sit upon
the farthest bench in the box of the figurantes.
It seemed to me as if I had got my foot just within
the theatre, although I had never yet been upon
the stage itself.

One night the little opera of the Two Little
Savoyards was given; in the market scene every
one, even the supernumeraries, might go up to
help in filling the stage; I heard them say so, and
rouging myself a little, I went happily up with the
others. I was in my ordinary dress; the confirmation coat, which still held together, although,
with regard to brushing and repairs, it looked but
miserably, and the great hat which fell down over
my face. I was very conscious of the ill condition
of my attire, and would have been glad to have
concealed it; but through the endeavour to do so,
my movements became still more angular. I did

not dare to hold myself upright, because, by doing so, I exhibited all the more plainly the shortness of my waistcoat, which I had outgrown. I had the feeling very plainly that people would make themselves merry about me; yet, at this moment, I felt nothing but the happiness of stepping for the first time before the foot-lamps. My heart beat; I stepped forward; there came up one of the singers, who at that time was much thought of, but now is forgotten; he took me by the hand, and jeeringly wished me happiness on my début. " Allow me to introduce you to the Danish public," said he, and drew me forward to the lamps. The people would laugh at me—I felt it; the tears rolled down my cheeks; I tore myself loose, and left the stage full of anguish.

Shortly after this, Dahlen arranged a ballet of Armida, in which I received a little part: I was a spirit. In this ballet I became acquainted with the lady of Professor Heiberg, the wife of the poet, and now a highly-esteemed actress on the Danish stage; she, then a little girl, had also a part in it, and our names stood printed in the bill. That was a moment in my life, when my name was printed! I fancied I could see in it a nimbus of immortality. I was continually looking at the printed paper. I carried the programme of the ballet with me at night to bed, lay and read my name by candle-light—in short, I was happy !

I had now been two years in Copenhagen. The sum of money which had been collected for me was expended, but I was ashamed of making known my wants and my necessities. I had removed to the house of a woman whose husband, when living, was master of a trading vessel, and there I had only lodging and breakfast. Those were heavy, dark days for me. The lady believed that I went out to dine with various families, whilst I only ate a little bread on one of the benches in the royal garden. Very rarely did I venture into some of the lowest eating-houses, and choose there the least expensive dish. I was, in truth, very forlorn ; but I did not feel the whole weight of my condition. Every person who spoke to me kindly I took for a faithful friend. God was with me in my little room ; and many a night, when I have said my evening prayer I asked of Him, like a child, "Will things soon be better with me ?" I had the notion, that as it went with me on New Year's Day, so it would go with me through the

whole year; and my highest wishes were to obtain
a part in a play.

It was now New Year's Day. The theatre was
closed, and only a half-blind porter sat at the entrance to the stage, on which there was not a soul.
I stole past him with beating heart, got between
the movable scenes and the curtain, and advanced
to the open part of the stage. Here I fell down
upon my knees, but not a single verse for declama-
tion could I recall to my memory. I then said
aloud the Lord's Prayer, and went out with the
persuasion, that because I had spoken from the
stage on New Year's Day, I should in the course
of the year succeed in speaking still more, as well
as in having a part assigned to me.

During the two years of my residence in Copenhagen I had never been out into the open country.
Once only had I been in the park, and there I had
been deeply engrossed by studying the diversions
of the people and their gay tumult. In the spring
of the third year, I went out for the first time
amid the verdure of a spring morning. It was
into the garden of the Fredricksberg, the summer
residence of Frederick VI. I stood still suddenly
under the first large budding beech tree. The

sun made the leaves transparent—there was a fragrance, a freshness—the birds sang. I was overcome by it—I shouted aloud for joy, threw my arms around the tree, and kissed it.

" Is he mad ?" said a man close behind me. It was one of the servants of the castle. I ran away, shocked at what I had heard, and then went thoughtfully and calmly back to the city.

My voice had, in the mean time, in part regained its richness. The singing master of the choir-school heard it, offered me a place in the school, thinking that, by singing with the choir, I should acquire greater freedom in the exercise of my powers on the stage. I thought that I could see by this means a new way opened for me. I went from the dancing-school into the singing-school, and entered the choir, now as a shepherd, and now as a warrior. The theatre was my world. I had permission to go in the pit, and thus it fared ill with my Latin. I heard many people say that there was no Latin required for singing in the choir, and that without the knowledge of this language it was possible to become a great actor. I thought there was good sense in that, and very often, either with or without reason, excused myself from my Latin evening lesson. Guldberg became aware of this, and for the first time I received a reprimand which almost crushed me to the earth. I fancy that no criminal could suffer more by hearing the sentence of death pronounced upon him. My distress of mind must have expressed itself in my countenance, for he said " Do not act any more comedy." But it was no comedy to me.

I was now to learn Latin no longer. I felt my dependence upon the kindness of others in such a degree as I had never done before. Occasionally I had had gloomy and earnest thoughts in looking forward to my future, because I was in want of the very necessaries of life; at other times I had the perfect thoughtlessness of a child.

The widow of the celebrated Danish statesman, Christian Colbjörnsen, and her daughter, were the first ladies of high rank who cordially befriended the poor lad; who listened to me with sympathy, and saw me frequently. Mrs. Colbjörnsen resided, during the summer, at Bakkehus, where also lived the poet Rahbek and his interesting wife. Rahbek never spoke to me; but his lively and kind-hearted wife often amused

herself with me. I had at that time again begun
to write a tragedy, which I read aloud to her.
Immediately on hearing the first scenes, she
exclaimed, "But you have actually taken whole
passages out of Oehlenschläger and Ingemann."

"Yes, but they are so beautiful!" replied I in
my simplicity, and read on.

One day, when I was going from her to Mrs.
Colbjörnsen, she gave me a handful of roses,
and said, "Will you take them up to her? It
will certainly give her pleasure to receive them
from the hand of a poet."

These words were said half in jest; but it was the
first time that any body had connected my name
with that of poet. It went through me, body and
soul, and tears filled my eyes. I know that from
this very moment, my mind was awoke to writing
and poetry. Formerly it had been merely an
amusement by way of variety from my puppet
theatre.

At Bakkehus lived also Professor Thiele, a
young student at that time, but even then the
editor of the Danish popular legends, and known
to the public as the solver of Baggesen's riddle,
and as the writer of beautiful poetry. He was

possessed of sentiment, true inspiration, and heart. He had calmly and attentively watched the unfolding of my mind, until we now became friends. He was one of the few who, at that time spoke the truth of me, when other people were making themselves merry at my expense, and having only eyes for that which was ludicrous in me. People had called me in jest, the little orator, and, as such, I was an object of curiosity. They found amusement in me, and I mistook every smile for a smile of applause. One of my later friends has told me that it probably was about this period that he saw me for the first time. It was in the drawing room of a rich tradesman, where people were making themselves very merry with me. They desired me to repeat one of my poems, and, as I did this with great feeling, the merriment was changed into sympathy with me.

I heard it said every day, what a good thing it would be for me if I could study. People advised me to devote myself to science, but no one moved one step to enable me to do so; it was labour enough for me to keep body and soul together. It therefore occurred to me to write a tragedy, which I would offer to the Theatre

Royal, and would then begin to study with the money which I should thus obtain. Whilst Guldberg instructed me in Danish, I had written a tragedy from a German story, called "The Chapel in the Wood;" yet as this was done merely as an exercise in the language, and, as he forbade me in the most decided manner to bring it out, I would not do so. I originated my own material, therefore; and within fourteen days I wrote my national tragedy called the "Robbers in Wissenberg" (the name of a little village in Funen). There was scarcely a word in it correctly written, as I had no person to help me, because I meant it to be anonymous; there was, nevertheless, one person admitted into the secret, namely, the young lady whom I had met with in Odense, during my preparation for confirmation, the only one who at that time showed me kindness and good-will. It was through her that I was introduced to the Colbjörnsen family, and thus known and received in all those circles of which the one leads into the other. She paid some one to prepare a legible copy of my piece, and undertook to present it for perusal. After an interval of six weeks, I received it back accompanied by a letter which said that people did not frequently wish to retain works which betrayed, in so great a degree, a want of elementary knowledge.

It was just at the close of the theatrical season, in May, 1823, that I received a letter from the directors, by which I was dismissed from the singing and dancing school, the letter adding also, that my participation in the school-teaching could lead to no advantage for me, but that they wished some of my many friends would enable me to receive an education, without which, talent availed nothing. I felt myself again, as it were, cast out into the wide world without help and without support. It was absolutely necessary that I should write a piece for the theatre, and that *must* be accepted; there was no other salvation for me. I wrote, therefore, a tragedy founded on a passage in history, and I called it "Alfsol." I was delighted with the first act, and with this I immediately went to the Danish translator of Shakspeare, Admiral Wulff, now deceased, who good-naturedly heard me read it. In after years I met with a most cordial reception in his family. At that time I also introduced myself to our celebrated physicist Oersted, and his house has remained to me to this day an affectionate home, to which my heart has firmly attached itself, and where I find my oldest and most unchangeable friends.

A favourite preacher, the rural dean Gutfeldt, was living at that time, and he it was who exerted himself most earnestly for my tragedy, which was now finished; and having written a letter of recommendation, he sent it to the managers of the theatre. I was suspended between hope and fear. In the course of the summer I endured bitter want, but I told it to no one, else many a one, whose sympathy I had experienced, would have helped me to the utmost of their means. A false shame prevented me from confessing what I had endured. Still happiness filled my heart. I read then for the first time the works of Walter Scott. A new world was opened to me: I forgot the reality, and gave to the circulating library that which should have provided me with a dinner.

The present conference councillor, Collin, one of the most distinguished men of Denmark, who unites with the greatest ability the noblest and best heart, to whom I looked up with confidence in all things, who has been a second father to me, and in whose children I have found brothers and sisters;—this excellent man I saw now for the first time. He was at that time director of the Theatre Royal, and people universally told me that it would be the best thing for me if he would interest himself on my behalf: it was either Oersted or Gutfeldt who first mentioned me to him; and now for the first time I went to that house which was to become so dear to me. Before the ramparts of Copenhagen were extended, this house lay outside the gate, and served as a summer residence to the Spanish Ambassador; now, however, it stands, a crooked, angular framework building, in a respectable street; an old-fashioned wooden balcony leads to the entrance, and a great tree spreads its green branches over the court and its pointed gables. It was to become a paternal house to me. Who does not willingly linger over the description of home?

I discovered only the man of business in Collin; his conversation was grave and in few words. I went away, without expecting any sympathy from this man; and yet it was precisely Collin who in all sincerity thought for my advantage, and who worked for it silently, as he had done for others, through the whole course of his active life. But at that time I did not understand the apparent calmness with which he listened, whilst his heart bled for the afflicted, and he always laboured for them with zeal and success, and knew how to help them. He touched so lightly upon my tragedy, which had been sent to him, and on account of which many people had overwhelmed me with flattering speeches, that I regarded him rather as an enemy than a protector.

In a few days I was sent for by the directors of the theatre, when Rahbek gave me back my play as useless for the stage; adding, however, that there were so many grains of corn scattered in it, that it was hoped, that perhaps, by earnest study, after going to school and the previous knowledge of all that is requisite, I might, some time, be able to write a work which should be worthy of being acted on the Danish stage.

In order therefore to obtain the means for my support and the necessary instruction, Collin recommended me to King Frederick the Sixth, who granted to me a certain sum annually for some years; and, by means of Collin also, the directors of the high schools allowed me to receive free instruction in the grammar school at Slagelse,

where, just then a new, and, as was said, an active
rector was appointed. I was almost dumb with
astonishment: never had I thought that my life
would take this direction, although I had no correct
idea of the path which I had now to tread. I was
to go with the earliest mail to Slagelse, which lay
twelve Danish miles from Copenhagen, to the
place where also the poets Baggesen and Ingemann
had gone to school. I was to receive money
quarterly from Collin; I was to apply to him in all
cases, and he it was who was to ascertain my
industry and my progress.

I went to him the second time to express to
him my thanks. Mildly and kindly he said to me,
" Write to me without restraint about every thing
which you require, and tell me how it goes with
you." From this hour I struck root in his heart,
no father could have been more to me than he was;
and is; none could have more heartily rejoiced in
my happiness, and my after reception with the
public; none have shared my sorrow more kindly;
and I am proud to say that one of the most excellent men which Denmark possesses feels towards
me as to his own child. His beneficence was
conferred without his making me feel it painful

either by word or by look. That was not the case
with every one to whom, in this change of my
fortunes, I had to offer my thanks; I was told to
think of my inconceivable happiness and my
poverty; in Collin's words was expressed the warm-
heartedness of a father, and to him it was that
properly I was indebted for every thing.

The journey was hastily determined upon, and
I had yet for myself some business to arrange. I
had spoken to an acquaintance from Odense who
had the management of a small printing concern
for a widow, to get "Alfsol" printed, that I might,
by the sale of the work, make a little money.
Before, however, the piece was printed, it was
necessary that I should obtain a certain number
of subscribers; but these were not obtained, and
the manuscript lay in the printing office, which, at
the time I went to fetch it away, was shut up.
Some years afterwards, however, it suddenly made
its appearance in print without my knowledge or
my desire, in its unaltered shape, but without my
name.

On a beautiful autumn day I set off with the
mail from Copenhagen to begin my school life in
Slagelse. A young student, who a month before

JONAS COLLIN
From a Painting by W. Marstrand
Engraved by E. C. W. Eckersberg, 1844

Jonas Collin.
From a Painting by W. Bendz.
Engraved by C. E. W. Sebaum, 1831.

had passed his first examination, and now was travelling home to Jutland to exhibit himself there as a student, and to see once more his parents and his friends, sate at my side and exalted for joy over the new life which now lay before him; he assured me that he should be the most unhappy of human beings if he were in my place, and were again beginning to go to the grammar school. But I travelled with a good heart towards the little city of Zealand. My mother received a joyful letter from me. I only wished that my father and the old grandmother yet lived, and could hear that I now went to the grammar school.

CHAPTER III

WHEN, late in the evening, I arrived at the inn in Slagelse, I asked the hostess if there were anything remarkable in the city.

"Yes," said she, "a new English fire-engine and Pastor Bastholm's library," and those probably were all the lions in the city. A few officers of the Lancers composed the fine-gentleman world. Everybody knew what was done in everybody's house, whether a scholar was elevated or degraded in his class, and the like. A private theatre, to which, at general rehearsal, the scholars of the grammar school and the maid-servants of the town had free entrance, furnished rich material for conversation. The place was remote from woods, and still farther from the coast; but the great post-road went through the city, and the post-horn resounded from the rolling carriage.

I boarded with a respectable widow of the

educated class, and had a little chamber looking out into the garden and field. My place in the school was in the lowest class, among little boys:— I knew indeed nothing at all.

I was actually like a wild bird which was confined in a cage; I had the greatest desire to learn, but for the moment I floundered about, as if I had been thrown into the sea; the one wave followed another, grammar, geography, mathematics— I felt myself overpowered by them, and feared that I should never be able to acquire all these. The rector, who took a peculiar delight in turning everything to ridicule, did not, of course, make an exception in my case. To me he stood there as a divinity; I believed unconditionally every word which he spoke. One day, when I had replied incorrectly to his question, and he said that I was stupid I mentioned it to Collin, and told him my anxiety, lest I did not deserve all that people had done for me; but he consoled me. Occasionally, however, on some subjects of instruction, I began to receive a good certificate, and the teachers were heartily kind to me; yet, notwithstanding that I advanced, I still lost confidence in myself more and more. On one of the first examinations, however,

I obtained the praise of the rector. He wrote the same in my character-book; and, happy in this, I went a few days afterwards to Copenhagen. Guldberg, who saw the progress I had made, received me kindly, and commended my zeal; and his brother in Odense furnished me the next summer with the means of visiting the place of my birth, where I had not been since I left it to seek adventures. I crossed the Belt, and went on foot to Odense. When I came near enough to see the lofty old church tower, my heart was more and more affected; I felt deeply the care of God for me, and I burst into tears. My mother rejoiced over me. The families of Iversen and Guldberg received me cordially; and in the little streets I saw the people open their windows to look after me, for everybody knew how remarkably well things had fared with me; nay, I felt that I actually stood upon the pinnacle of fortune, when one of the principal citizens, who had built a high tower to his house, led me up there, and I looked out thence over the city and the surrounding country and some old women in the hospital below, who had known me from childhood, pointed up to me.

As soon, however, as I returned to Slagelse,

this halo of glory vanished, as well as every thought
of it. I may freely confess that I was industrious,
and I rose, as soon as it was possible, into a higher
class; but in proportion as I rose did I feel the
pressure upon me more strongly, and that my
endeavours were not sufficiently productive. Many
an evening, when sleep overcame me, did I wash
my head with cold water, or run about the lonely
little garden, till I was again wakeful, and could
comprehend the book anew. The rector filled up
a portion of his hours of teaching with jests, nick-
names, and not the happiest of witticisms. I was
as if paralysed with anxiety when he entered the
room, and from that cause my replies often
expressed the opposite of that which I wished to
say, and thereby my anxiety was all the more
increased. What was to become of me ?

In a moment of ill humour I wrote a letter to
the head master, who was one of those who was
most cordially opposed to me. I said in this
letter that I regarded myself as a person so little
gifted by nature, that it was impossible for me to
study, and that the people in Copenhagen threw
away the money which they spent upon me: I
besought him therefore to counsel me what I

should do. The excellent man strengthened me with mild words, and wrote to me a most friendly and consolatory letter; he said that the rector meant kindly by me—that it was his custom and way of acting—that I was making all the progress that people could expect from me, and that I need not doubt of my abilities. He told me that he himself was a peasant youth of three and twenty, older than I myself was, when he began his studies; the misfortune for me was, that I ought to have been treated differently to the other scholars, but that this could hardly be done in a school, but that things were progressing, and that I stood well both with the teachers and my fellow students.

Every Sunday we had to attend the church and hear an old preacher; the other scholars learned their lessons in history and mathematics while he preached; I learned my task in religion, and thought that, by so doing, it was less sinful. The general rehearsals at the private theatre were points of light in my school life; they took place in a back building, where the lowing of the cows might be heard; the street-decoration was a picture of the market-place of the city, by which means the representation had something familiar about it; it amused the inhabitants to see their own houses.

On Sunday afternoons it was my delight to go to the castle of Antvorskov, at that time only half ruinous, and once a monastery, where I pursued the excavating of the ruined cellars, as if it had been a Pompeii. I also often rambled to the Crucifix of St. Anders, which stands upon one of the heights of Slagelse, and which is one of the wooden crosses erected in the time of Catholicism in Denmark. St. Anders was a priest in Slagelse, and travelled to the Holy Land; on the last day he remained so long praying on the holy grave, that the ship sailed away without him. Vexed at this circumstance, he walked along the shore, where a man met him riding on an ass, and took him up with him. Immediately he fell asleep, and when he awoke he heard the bells of Slagelse ringing. He lay upon the (Hvilehöi) hill of rest, where the cross now stands. He was at home a year and a day before the ship returned, which had sailed away without him, and an angel had borne him home. The legend, and the place where he woke, were both favourites of mine. From this spot I could see the ocean and Funen. Here I could indulge my fancies; when at home, my sense of duty chained my thoughts only to my books.

The happiest time, however, was when, once on a Sunday, whilst the wood was green, I went to the city of Sorö, two (Danish) miles from Slagelse, and which lies in the midst of woods, surrounded by lakes. Here is an academy for the nobility, founded by the poet Holberg. Every thing lay in a conventional stillness. I visited here the poet Ingemann, who had just married, and who held a situation as teacher; he had already received me kindly in Copenhagen; but here his reception of me was still more kind. His life in this place seemed to me like a beautiful story; flowers and vines twined around his window; the rooms were adorned with the portraits of distinguished poets, and other pictures. We sailed upon the lake with an Æolian harp made fast to the mast. Ingemann talked so cheerfully, and his excellent, amiable wife treated me as if she were an elder sister:—I loved these people. Our friendship has grown with years. I have been from that time almost every summer a welcome guest there, and I have experienced that there are people in whose society one is made better, as it were; that which is bitter passes away, and the whole world appears in sunlight.

Among the pupils in the academy of nobles, there were two who made verses; they knew that I did the same, and they attached themselves to me. The one was Petit, who afterwards, certainly with the best intention, but not faithfully, translated several of my books; the other, the poet Carl Bagger, one of the most gifted of men who has come forward in Danish literature, but who has been unjustly judged. His poems are full of freshness and originality; his story, "The Life of my Brother," is a clever book, by the critique on which the Danish Monthly Review of Literature has proved that it does not understand how to give judgment. These two academicians were very different from me : life rushed rejoicingly through their veins; I was sensitive and childlike.

In my character-book I always received, as regarded my conduct, "remarkably good." On one occasion, however, I only obtained the testimony of "very good;" and so anxious and childlike was I, that I wrote a letter to Collin on that account, and assured him in grave earnestness, that I was perfectly innocent, although I had only obtained a character of " very good."

The rector grew weary of his residence in Slagelse; he applied for the vacant post of rector in the grammar school of Helsingör, and obtained it. He told me of it, and added kindly, that I might write to Collin and ask leave to accompany him thither; that I might live in his house, and could even now remove to his family; I should then in half a year become a student, which could not be the case if I remained behind, and that then he would himself give me some private lessons in Latin and Greek. On this same occasion he wrote also to Collin; and this letter, which I afterwards saw, contained the greatest praise of my industry, of the progress I had made, and of my good abilities, which last I imagined that he thoroughly mistook, and for the want of which, I myself had so often wept. I had no conception that he judged of me so favourably; it would have strengthened and relieved me had I known it; whereas, on the contrary, his perpetual blame depressed me. I, of course, immediately received Collin's permission, and removed to the house of the rector. But that, alas! was an unfortunate house.

I accompanied him to Helsingör, one of the lovliest places in Denmark, close to the Sound, which is at this place not above a mile (Danish) broad, and which seems like a blue, swelling river between Denmark and Sweden. The ships of all nations sail past daily by hundreds; in winter the ice forms a firm bridge between the two countries, and when in spring this breaks up, it resembles a floating glacier. The scenery here made a lively impression upon me, but I dared only to cast stolen glances at it. When the school hours were over, the house door was commonly locked; I was obliged to remain in the heated school-room and learn my Latin, or else play with the children, or sit in my little room; I never went out to visit anybody. My life in this family furnishes the most evil dreams to my remembrance. I was almost overcome by it, and my prayer to God every evening was, that He would remove this cup from me and let me die. I possessed not an atom of confidence in myself. I never mentioned in my letters how hard it went with me, because the rector found his pleasure in making a jest of me, and turning my feelings to ridicule. I never complained of any one, with the exception of myself. I knew that they would say in Copenhagen, "He has not the desire to do any thing; a fanciful being can do no good with realities."

My letters to Collin, written at this time, showed such a gloomy despairing state of mind, that they touched him deeply; but people imagined that was not to be helped; they fancied that it was my disposition, and not, as was the case, that it was the consequence of outward influences. My temper of mind was thoroughly buoyant, and susceptible of every ray of sunshine; but only on one single holiday in the year, when I could go to Copenhagen, was I able to enjoy it.

What a change it was to get for a few days out of the rector's rooms into a house in Copenhagen, where all was elegance, cleanliness, and full of the comforts of refined life! This was at Admiral Wulff's, whose wife felt for me the kindness of a mother, and whose children met me with cordiality; they dwelt in a portion of the Castle of Amalienburg, and my chamber looked out into the square. I remember the first evening there; Alladin's words passed through my mind, when he looked down from his splendid castle into the square, and said, "Here came I as a poor lad."— My soul was full of gratitude.

During my whole residence in Slagelse I had scarcely written more than four or five poems; two of which, "The Soul," and "To my Mother," will be found printed in my collected works. During my school-time at Helsingör I wrote only one single poem, "The Dying Child;" a poem which, of all my after works became most popular and most widely circulated. I read it to some acquaintance in Copenhagen; some were struck by it, but most of them only remarked my Funen dialect, which drops the d in every word. I was commended by many; but from the greater number I received a lecture on modesty, and that I should not get too great ideas of myself—I who really at that time thought nothing of myself.*

At the house of Admiral Wulff I saw many men of the most distinguished talent, and among them all my mind paid the greatest homage to one— that was the poet Adam Oehlenschläger. I heard his praise resound from every mouth around me ; I looked up to him with the most pious faith : I was happy when one evening, in a large brilliantly-lighted drawing room—where I deeply felt that my

* How beautifully is all this part of the author's experience reflected in that of Antonio, the Improvisatore, whose highly sensitive nature was too often wounded by the well-meant lectures of patrons and commonplace minds.—M.H.

apparel was the shabbiest there, and for that reason I concealed myself behind the long curtains—Oehlenschläger came to me and offered me his hand. I could have fallen before him on my knees. I again saw Weyse, and heard him improvise upon the piano. Wulff himself read aloud his translations of Byron; and Oehlenschläger's young daughter Charlotte surprised me by her joyous, merry humour.

From such a house as this, I, after a few days, returned to the rector, and felt the difference deeply. He also came direct from Copenhagen, where he had heard it said that I had read in company one of my own poems. He looked at me with penetrating glance, and commanded me to bring him the poem, when, if he found in it one spark of poetry, he would forgive me. I tremblingly brought to him "The Dying Child;" he read it, and pronounced it to be sentimentality and idle trash. He gave way freely to his anger. If he had believed that I wasted my time in writing verses, or that I was of a nature which required a severe treatment, then his intention would have been good ; but he could not pretend this. But from this day forward my situation was more unfortunate than ever ; I suffered so severely in my mind that I was nearly sinking under it. That was the darkest, the most unhappy time in my life.

Just then one of the masters went to Copenhagen, and related to Collin exactly what I had to bear, and immediately he removed me from the school and from the rector's house. When, in taking leave of him, I thanked him for the kindness which I had received from him, the passionate man cursed me, and ended by saying that I should never become a student, that my verses would grow mouldy on the floor of the bookseller's shop, and that I myself should end my days in a mad-house. I trembled to my innermost being, and left him.

Several years afterwards, when my writings were read, when the Improvisatore first came out, I met him in Copenhagen; he offered me his hand in a conciliatory manner, and said that he had erred respecting me, and had treated me wrong ; but it now was all the same to me. The heavy, dark days had also produced their blessing in my life.

A young man, who afterwards became cele-brated in Denmark for his zeal in the Northern

languages and in history, became my teacher. I
hired a little garret; it is described in the Fiddler;
and in The Picture Book without Pictures, people
may see that I often received there visits from the
moon. I had a certain sum allowed for my
support; but as instruction was to be paid for, I
had to make savings in other ways. A few families through the week-days gave me a place at
their tables. I was a sort of boarder, as many
another poor student in Copenhagen is still: there
was a variety in it; it gave an insight into the several kinds of family life, which was not without
influence on me. I studied industriously; in some
particular branches I had considerably distinguished myself in Helsingör, especially in mathematics; these were, therefore, now much more
left to myself: every thing tended to assist me in
my Greek and Latin studies; in one direction,
however, and that the one in which it would least
have been expected, did my excellent teacher
find much to do; namely, in religion. He closely
adhered to the literal meaning of the Bible; with
this I was acquainted, because from my first
entrance in the school I had clearly understood
what was said and taught by it. I received gladly,

both with feeling and understanding, the doctrine, that God is love : every thing which opposed this—a burning hell, therefore, whose fire endured for ever—I could not recognise. Released from the distressing existence of the school-bench, I now expressed myself like a free man; and my teacher, who was one of the noblest and most amiable of human beings, but who adhered firmly to the letter, was often quite distressed about me. We disputed, whilst pure flames kindled within our hearts. It was nevertheless good for me that I came to this unspoiled, highly-gifted young man, who was possessed of a nature as peculiar as my own.

That which, on the contrary, was an error in me, and which became very perceptible, was a pleasure which I had, not in jesting with, but in playing with my best feelings, and in regarding the understanding as the most important thing in the world. The rector had completely mistaken my undisguisedly candid and sensitive character; my excitable feelings were made ridiculous, and thrown back upon themselves ; and now, when I could freely advance upon the way to my object, this change showed itself in me. From severe suffering I did not rush into libertinism, but into an erroneous endeavour to appear other than I was. I ridiculed feeling, and fancied that I had quite thrown it aside; and yet I could be made wretched for a whole day, if I met with a sour countenance where I expected a friendly one. Every poem which I had formerly written with tears, I now parodied, or gave to it a ludicrous refrain; one of which I called " The Lament of the Kitten," another, "The Sick Poet." The few poems which I wrote at that time were all of a humorous character: a complete change had passed over me; the stunted plant was reset, and now began to put forth new shoots.

Wulff's eldest daughter, a very clever and lively girl, understood and encouraged the humour, which made itself evident in my few poems; she possessed my entire confidence she protected me like a good sister, and had great influence over me, whilst she awoke in me a feeling for the comic.

At this time also, a fresh current of life was sent through the Danish literature; for this the people had an interest, and politics played no part in it.

Heiberg, who had gained the acknowledged reputation of a poet by his excellent works,

"Psyche" and "Walter the Potter," had introduced the vaudeville, upon the Danish stage ; it
was a Danish vaudeville, blood of our blood, and
was therefore received with acclamation, and
supplanted almost every thing else. Thalia kept
carnival on the Danish stage, and Heiberg was her
secretary. I made his acquaintance first at
Oersted's. Refined, eloquent, and the hero of the
day, he pleased me in a high degree: he was most
kind to me, and I visited him; he considered one of
my humourous poems worthy of a place in his
most excellent weekly paper, "The Flying Post."
Shortly before I had, after a deal of trouble, got my
poem of "The Dying Child" printed in a paper;
none of the many publishers of journals, who
otherwise accept of the most lamentable trash, had
the courage to print a poem by a schoolboy. My
best known poem they printed at that time,
accompanied by an excuse for it. Heiberg saw
it, and gave it in his paper an honourable place.
Two humourous poems, signed H., were truly my
début with him.

I remember the first evening when the "Flying
Post" appeared with my verses in it. I was with
a family who wished me well, but who regarded my

poetical talent as quite insignificant, and who found something to censure in every line. The master of the house entered with the "Flying Post" in his hand.

"This evening," said he, "there are two excellent poems: they are by Heiberg; nobody else could write anything like them." And now my poems were received with rapture. The daughter, who was in my secret exclaimed, in her delight, that I was the author. They were all struck into silence, and were vexed. That wounded me deeply.

One of our least esteemed writers, but a man of rank, who was very hospitable, gave me one day a seat at his table. He told me that a new year's gift would come out, and that he was applied to for a contribution I said that a little poem of mine, at the wish of the publisher, would appear in the same new year's gift.

"What then, everybody and anybody are to contribute to this book!" said the man in vexation: "then he will need nothing from me; I certainly can hardly give him anything."

My teacher dwelt at a considerable distance from me. I went to him twice each day, and on the way there my thoughts were occupied with my lessons. On my return, however, I breathed more freely, and then bright poetical ideas passed through my brain, but they were never committed to paper; only five or six humorous poems were written in the course of the year, and these disturbed me less when they were laid to rest on paper than if they had remained in my mind.

In September, 1828, I was a student; and when the examination was over, the thousand ideas and thoughts, by which I was pursued on the way to my teacher, flew like a swarm of bees out into the world, and indeed into my first work, "A Journey, on Foot to Amack;" a peculiar, humorous book, but one which fully exhibited my own individual character at that time, my disposition to sport with every thing, and to jest in tears over my own feelings—a fantastic, gaily-coloured tapestry-work. No publisher had the courage to bring out that little book; I therefore ventured to do it myself, and, in a few days after its appearance, the impression was sold. Publisher Reitzel bought from me the second edition; after a while he had a third; and besides this, the work was reprinted in Sweden.

Every body read my book; I heard nothing but

praise; I was "a student,"—I had attained the highest goal of my wishes. I was in a whirl of joy; and in this state I wrote my first dramatic work, "Love on the Nicholas Tower, or, What says the Pit?" It was unsuccessful, because it satirised that which no longer existed amongst us, namely, the shows of the middle ages; besides which, it rather ridiculed the enthusiasm for the vaudeville. The subject of it was, in short, as follows:—The watchman of the Nicholas Tower, who always spoke as a knight of the castle, wished to give his daughter to the watchman of the neighbouring church tower; but she loved a young tailor, who had made a journey to the grave of Eulenspiegel, and was just now returned, as the punch-bowl steamed, and was to be emptied in honour of the young lady's consent being given. The lovers escaped together to the tailor's herberg, where dancing and merriment is going forward. The watchman, however, fetches back his daughter; but she had lost her senses, and she assured them that she never would recover them, unless she had her tailor. The old watchman determines that Fate should decide the affair; but, then, who was Fate? The idea then comes into his head that the public shall be his Pythia, and that the public shall decide whether she should have the tailor or the watchman. They determine, therefore, to send to one of the youngest of the poets, and beg him to write the history in the style of the vaudeville, a kind of writing which was the most successful at that time, and when the piece was brought upon the stage, and the public either whistled or hissed, it should be in no wise considered that the work of the young author had been unsuccessful, but that it should be the voice of Fate, which said, "She shall marry the watchman." If on the contrary, the piece was successful, it indicated that she should have the tailor; and this last, remarked the father, must be said in prose, in order that the public may understand it. Now every one of the characters thought himself on the stage, where in the epilogue the lovers besought the public for their applause, whilst the watchman begged them either to whistle, or at least to hiss.

My fellow students received the piece with acclamation; they were proud of me. I was the second of their body who in this year had brought out a piece on the Danish stage; the other was Arnesen, student at the same time with me, and author of a vaudeville called " The Intrigue in the People's Theatre," a piece which had a great run. We were the two young authors of the October examination, two of the sixteen poets which this year produced, and whom people in jest divided into the four great and the twelve small poets.

I was now a happy human being ; I possessed the soul of a poet, and the heart of youth ; all houses began to open to me ; I flew from circle to circle. Still, however, I devoted myself industriously to study, so that in September, 1829, I passed my *Examen philologicum et philosophicum*, and brought out the first collected edition of my poems, which met with great praise. Life lay bright with sunshine before me.

CHAPTER IV

UNTIL now I had only seen a small part of my native land, that is to say, a few points in Funen and Zealand, as well as Moen's Klint, which last is truly one of our most beautiful places; the beech-woods there hang like a garland over the white chalk cliffs, from which a view is obtained far over the Baltic. I wished, therefore, in the summer of 1830, to devote my first literary proceeds to seeing Jutland, and making myself more thoroughly acquainted with my own Funen. I had no idea how much solidity of mind I should derive from this summer excursion, or what a change was about to take place in my inner life.

Jutland, which stretches between the German Ocean and the Baltic, until it ends at Skagen in a reef of quicksands, possesses a peculiar character. Towards the Baltic extend immense woods and hills; towards the North Sea, mountains and quicksands, scenery of a grand and solitary charac-ter; and between the two, infinite expanses of brown heath, with their wandering gipsies, their

wailing birds, and their deep solitude, which the
Danish poet, Steen Blicher, has described in his
novels.

This was the first foreign scenery which I had
ever seen, and the impression, therefore, which it
made upon me was very strong.* In the cities,
where my "Journey on Foot" and my comic
poems were known, I met with a good reception.
Funen revealed her rural life to me; and, not far
from my birth-place of Odense, I passed several
weeks at the country seat of the elder Iversen as a
welcome guest. Poems sprung forth upon paper,
but of the comic fewer and fewer. Sentiment,
which I had so often derided, would now be avenged.
I arrived, in the course of my journey, at the
house of a rich family in a small city; and here
suddenly a new world opened before me, an immense world, which yet could be contained in four
lines, which I wrote at that time :—

> A pair of dark eyes fixed my sight,
> They were my world, my home, my delight,
> The soul beamed in them, and childlike peace,
> And never on earth will their memory cease.

* This impressive and wild scenery with its characteristic figures
of gipsies etc., is most exquisitely introduced into the authors novel
of "O T.;"—indeed it gives a colouring and tone to the whole work,
which the reader never can forget. In my opinion Andersen never
wrote anything finer in the way of description than many parts of
this work, though as a story it is not equal to his others.—M H.

New plans of life occupied me. I would give
up writing poetry,—to what could it lead? I
would study theology, and become a preacher; I
had only one thought, and that was *she*. But
it was self-delusion: she loved another; she married him. It was not till several years later that I
felt and acknowledged that it was best, both for
her and for myself, that things had fallen out as
they were. She had no idea, perhaps, how deep
my feeling for her had been, or what an influence
it produced in me. She had become the excellent
wife of a good man, and a happy mother. God's
blessing rest upon her!

In my "Journey on Foot," and in most of my
writings, satire had been the prevailing characteristic. This displeased many people, who thought
that this bent of mind could lead to no good purpose. The critics now blamed me precisely for
that which a far deeper feeling had expelled from
my breast. A new collection of Poetry, "Fancies
and Sketches," which was published for the new
year, showed satisfactorily what my heart suffered.
A paraphrase of the history of my own heart
appeared in a serious vaudeville, "Parting and
Meeting," with this difference only, that here the

love was mutual: the piece was not presented on the stage till five years later.

Among my young friends in Copenhagen at that time was Orla Lehmann, who afterwards rose higher in popular favour, on account of his political efforts, than any man in Denmark. Full of animation, eloquent and undaunted, his character of mind was one which interested me also. The German language was much studied at his father's; they had received there Heine's poems, and they were very attractive for young Orla. He lived in the country, in the neighbourhood of the castle of Fredricksberg. I went there to see him, and he sang as I came one of Heine's verses, "Thalatta, Thalatta, du eviges Meer." We read Heine together; the afternoon and the evening passed, and I was obliged to remain there all night; but I had on this evening made the acquaintance of a poet, who, as it seemed to me, sang from the soul; he supplanted Hoffman, who, as might be seen by my "Journey on Foot," had formerly had the greatest influence on me. In my youth there were only three authors who as it were infused themselves into my blood,—Walter Scott, Hoffman, and Heine.

I betrayed more and more in my writings an unhealthy turn of mind. I felt an inclination to seek for the melancholy in life, and to linger on the dark side of things; I became sensitive, and thought rather of the blame than the praise which was lavished on me. My late school education, which was forced, and my impulse to become an author whilst I was yet a student, make it evident that my first work, the " Journey on Foot," was not without grammatical errors. Had I only paid some one to correct the press, which was a work I was unaccustomed to, then no charge of this kind could have been brought against me. Now, on the contrary, people laughed at these errors, and dwelt upon them, passing over carelessly that in the book which had merit. I know people who only read my poems to find out errors; they noted down, for instance, how often I used the word *beautiful*, or some similar word. A gentleman, now a clergyman, at that time a writer of vaude-villes and a critic, was not ashamed, in a company where I was, to go through several of my poems in this style; so that a little girl of six years old, who heard with amazement that he discovered every thing to be wrong, took the book, and pointing out the conjunction *and*, said, " There is yet a little word about which you have not scolded." He felt what a reproof lay in the remark of the child; he looked ashamed and kissed the little one. All this wounded me; but I had, since my school-days, become somewhat timid, and that caused me to take it all quietly: I was morbidly sensitive, and I was good-natured to a fault. Everybody knew it, and some were on that account almost cruel to me. Every body wished to teach me; almost every body said that I was spoiled by praise, and therefore *they* would speak the truth to me. Thus I heard continually of my faults, the real and the ideal weaknesses. In the mean time, however, my feelings burst forth; and then I said that I would become a poet whom they should see honoured. But this was regarded only as the crowning mark of the most unbearable vanity; and from house to house it was repeated. I was a good man, they said, but one of the vainest in existence; and in that very time I was often ready wholly to despair of my abilities, and had, as in the darkest days of my school-life, a feeling, as if my whole talent were a self-deception. I almost believed so ; but it was more than I could bear, to hear the same thing said, sternly and jeeringly, by others; and if I then uttered a proud, an inconsiderate word, it was addressed to the scourge with which I was smitten; and when those who smite are those we love, then do the scourges become scorpions.

For this reason Collin thought that I should make a little journey,—for instance, to North Germany,—in order to divert my mind and furnish me with new ideas.

In the spring of 1831, I left Denmark for the first time. I saw Lübeck and Hamburg. Everything astonished me and occupied my mind. I saw mountains for the first time,—the Harzgebirge. The world expanded so astonishingly before me. My good humour returned to me, as to the bird of passage. Sorrow is the flock of sparrows which remains behind, and builds in the nests of the birds of passage. But I did not feel myself wholly restored.

In Dresden I made acquaintance with Tieck. Ingemann had given me a letter to him. I heard him one evening read aloud one of Shakspeare's plays. On taking leave of him, he wished me a poet's success, embraced and kissed me; which made the deepest impression upon me. The expression of his eyes I shall never forget. I left him with tears, and prayed most fervently to God for strength to enable me to pursue the way after which my whole soul strove—strength, which should enable me to express that which I felt in my soul; and that when I next saw Tieck, I might be known and valued by him. It was not until several years afterwards, when my later works were translated into German, and well received in his country, that we saw each other again; I felt the true hand-pressure of him who had given to me, in my second fatherland, the kiss of consecration.

In Berlin, a letter of Oersted's procured me the acquaintance of Chamisso. That grave man, with his long locks and honest eyes, opened the door to me himself, read the letter, and I know not how it was, but we understood each other immediately. I felt perfect confidence in him, and told him so, though it was in bad German. Chamisso understood Danish; I gave him my poems, and he was the first who translated any of them, and thus introduced me into Germany. It was thus he spoke of me at that time in the *Morgenblatt*:

" Gifted with wit, fancy, humour, and a national naïveté, Andersen has still in his power tones which awaken deeper echoes. He understands, in particular, how with perfect ease, by a few slight but graphic touches, to call into existence little pictures of landscapes, but which are often so peculiarly local as not to interest those who are unfamiliar with the home of the poet. Perhaps that which may be translated from him, or which is so already, may be the least calculated to give a proper idea of him."

Chamisso became a friend for my whole life. The pleasure which he had in my later writings may be seen by the printed letters addressed to me in the collected edition of his works.

The little journey in Germany had great influence upon me, as my Copenhagen friends acknowledged. The impressions of the journey were immediately written down, and I gave them forth under the title of "Shadow Pictures." Whether I were actually improved or not, there still prevailed at home the same petty pleasure in dragging out my faults, the same perpetual schooling of me ; and I was weak enough to endure it from those who were officious meddlers. I seldom made a joke of it; but if I did so, it was called **arrogance and vanity**, and it was asserted that I never would listen to rational people. Such an instructor once asked me whether I wrote *Dog* with a little *d*,"—he had found such an error of the press in my last work. I replied, jestingly, " Yes, because I here spoke of a little dog."

But these are small troubles, people will say. Yes, but they are drops which wear hollows in the rock. I speak of it here; I feel a necessity to do so; here to protest against the accusation of vanity, which, since no other error can be discovered in my private life, is seized upon, and even now is thrown at me like an old medal.

From the end of the year 1828, to the beginning of 1839, I maintained myself alone by my writings. Denmark is a small country; but few books at that time went to Sweden and Norway; and on that account the profit could not be great. It was difficult for me to pull through,—doubly difficult, because my dress must in some measure accord with the circles into which I went. To produce, and always to be producing was destructive, nay, impossible. I translated a few pieces for the theatre,—*La Quarantaine*, and *La Reine de seize ans*; and as, at that time, a young composer of the name of Hartmann, a grandson of him who composed the Danish folks-song of "King Christian stood by the tall, tall mast," wished for text to an opera, I was of course ready to write it. Through the writings of Hoffman, my attention had been turned to the masked comedies of Gozzi: I read *Il Corvo*, and finding that it was an excellent subject, I wrote, in a few weeks, my opera-text of the Raven. It will sound strange to the ears of my countrymen when I say that I, at that time, recommended Hartmann; that *I* gave my word for it, in my letter to the theatrical directors, for his being a man of talent, who would produce something good. He now takes the first rank among the living Danish composers.

I worked up also Walter Scott's "Bride of Lammermoor" for another young composer, Bredal. Both operas appeared on the stage; but I was subjected to the most merciless criticism, as one who had stultified the labours of foreign poets. What people had discovered to be good in me before seemed to be now forgotten, and all talent was denied to me. The composer Weyse, my earliest benefactor, whom I have already mentioned,

was, on the contrary, satisfied in the highest
degree with my treatment of these subjects.
He told me that he had wished for a long time to
compose an opera from Walter Scott's "Kenil-
worth." He now requested me to commence the
joint work, and write the text. I had no idea of
the summary justice which would be dealt to me.
I needed money to live, and, what still more determined me to it, I felt flattered to have to work
with Weyse, our most celebrated composer. It
delighted me that he, who had first spoken in my
favour at Siboni's house, now, as artist, sought a
noble connection with me. I had scarcely half
finished the text, when I was already blamed for
having made use of a well-known romance. I
wished to give it up; but Weyse consoled me, and
encouraged me to proceed. Afterwards, before
he had finished the music, when I was about to
travel abroad, I committed my fate, as regarded
the text, entirely to his hands. He wrote whole
verses of it, and the altered conclusion is wholly
his own. It was a peculiarity of that singular man
that he liked no book which ended sorrowfully.
For that reason, Amy must marry Leicester, and
Elizabeth say, " Proud England, I am thine." I

opposed this at the beginning; but afterwards I yielded, and the piece was really half created by Weyse. It was brought on the stage, but was not printed, with the exception of the songs. To this followed anonymous attacks: the city post brought me letters in which the unknown writers scoffed at and derided me. That same year I published a new collection of poetry, ",The Twelve Months of the Year;" and this book, though it was afterwards pronounced to contain the greater part of the best lyrical poems, was then condemned as bad.

At that time "The Monthly Review of Literature," though it is now gone to its grave, was in its full bloom. At its first appearance, it numbered among its co-workers some of the most distinguished names. Its want, however, was men who were qualified to speak ably on æsthetic works. Unfortunately, everybody fancies himself able to give an opinion upon these; but people may write excellently on surgery or pedagogical science, and may have a name in those things, and yet be dolts in poetry: of this proofs may be seen. By degrees it became more and more difficult for the critical bench to find a judge for poetical works. The one, however, who, through his extraordinary zeal for

writing and speaking, was ready at hand, was the
historian and states-councillor Molbech, who
played, in our time, so great a part in the history
of Danish criticism, that I must speak of him
rather more fully. He is an industrious collector,
writes extremely correct Danish, and his Danish
dictionary, let him be reproached with whatever
want he may, is a most highly useful work ; but, as
a judge of æsthetic works, he is one-sided, and even
fanatically devoted to party spirit. He belongs,
unfortunately, to the men of science, who are only
one sixty-fourth of a poet, and who are the most
incompetent judges of æsthetics. He has, for
example, by his critiques on Ingemann's romances,
shown how far he is below the poetry which he
censures. He has himself published a volume of
poems, which belong to the common run of books,
"A Ramble through Denmark," written in the *fade*
flowery style of those times, and "A Journey
through Germany, France, and Italy," which
seem to be made up out of books, not out of life.
He sate in his study, or in the Royal Library,
where he has a post, when suddenly he became
director of the theatre and censor of the pieces
sent in. He was sickly, one-sided in judgment,

and irritable: people may imagine the result. He spoke of my first poems very favourably; but my star soon sank for another, who was in the ascendant, a young lyrical poet, Paludan Müller; and, as he no longer loved, he hated me. That is the short history; indeed in the selfsame Monthly Review the very poems which had formerly been praised were now condemned by the same judge, when they appeared in a new increased edition. There is a Danish proverb, "When the carriage drags, everybody pushes behind;" and I proved the truth of it now.

It happened that a new star in Danish literature ascended at this time. Henrik Hertz published his "Letters from the Dead" anonymously: it was a mode of driving all the unclean things out of the temple. The deceased Baggesen sent polemical letters from Paradise, which resembled in the highest degree the style of that author. They contained a sort of apotheosis of Heiberg, and in part attacks upon Oehlenschläger and Hauch. The old story about my orthographical errors was again revived; my name and my school days in Slagelse were brought into connection with St. Anders. I was ridiculed, or, if people will, I was chastised.

Hertz's book went through all Denmark; people spoke of nothing but him. It made it still more piquant that the author of the work could not be discovered. People were enraptured, and justly. Heiberg, in his "Flying Post," defended a few æsthetical insignificants, but not me. I felt the wound of the sharp knife deeply. My enemies now regarded me as entirely shut out from the world of spirits. I however in a short time published a little book, "Vignettes to the Danish Poets," in which I characterised the dead and the living authors in a few lines each, but only spoke of that which was good in them. The book excited attention : it was regarded as one of the best of my works ; it was imitated, but the critics did not meddle with it. It was evident, on this occasion, as had already been the case, that the critics never laid hands on those of my works which were the most successful.

My affairs were now in their worst condition ; and precisely in that same year in which a stipend for travelling had been conferred upon Hertz, I also had presented a petition for the same purpose. The universal opinion was that I had reached the point of culmination, and if I was to succeed in travelling it must be at this present time. I felt, what since then has become an acknowledged fact, that travelling would be the best school for me. In the mean time I was told that to bring it under consideration I must endeavour to obtain from the most distinguished poets and men of science a kind of recommendation; because this very year there were so many young men who were soliciting a stipend, that it would be difficult among these to put in an available claim. I therefore obtained recommendations for myself; and I am, so far as I know the only Danish poet who was obliged to produce recommendations to prove that he was a poet. And here also it is remarkable, that the men who recommended me have each one made prominent some very different qualification which gave me a claim: for instance, Oehlenschläger, my lyrical power, and the earnestness that was in me; Ingemann, my skill in depicting popular life; Heiberg declared that, since the days of Wessel, no Danish poet had possessed so much humour as myself; Oersted remarked, every one, they who were against me as well as those who were for me, agreed on one subject, and this was that I was a *true*

poet. Thiele expressed himself warmly and en-
thusiastically about the power which he had seen
in me, combating against the oppression and the
misery of life. I received a stipend for travelling;
Hertz a larger and I a smaller one: and that also
was quite in the order of things.

"Now be happy," said my friends, " make
yourself aware of your unbounded good fortune!
Enjoy the present moment, as it will probably be
the only time in which you will get abroad. You
shall hear what people say about you while you
are travelling, and how we shall defend you; sometimes, however, we shall not be able to do that."

It was painful to me to hear such things said;
I felt a compulsion of soul to be away, that I
might, if possible, breathe freely; but sorrow is
firmly seated on the horse of the rider. More than
one sorrow oppressed my heart, and although I
opened the chambers of my heart to the world,
one or two of them I keep locked, nevertheless.
On setting out on my journey, my prayer to God
was that I might die far away from Denmark, or
return strengthened for activity, and in a condition to produce works which should win for me
and my beloved ones joy and honour.

Precisely at the moment of setting out on my journey, the form of my beloved arose in my heart. Among the few whom I have already named, there are two who exercised a great influence upon my life and my poetry, and these I must more particularly mention. A beloved mother, an unusually liberal-minded and well educated lady, Madame Lässöe, had introduced me into her agreeable circle of friends; she often felt the deepest sympathy with me in my troubles; she always turned my attention to the beautiful in nature and the poetical in the details of life, and as almost every one regarded me as a poet, she elevated my mind; yes, and if there be tenderness and purity in anything which I have written, they are among those things which I have especially to be thankful to her. Another character of great importance to me was Collin's son Edward. Brought up under fortunate circumstances of life, he was possessed of that courage and determination which I wanted. I felt that he sincerely loved me, and I, full of affection, threw myself upon him with my whole soul; he passed on calmly and practically through the business of life. I often mistook him at the very moment when he

felt for me most deeply, and when he would gladly
have infused into me a portion of his own character,
—to me who was as a reed shaken by the wind.
In the practical part of life, he, the younger, stood
actively by my side, from the assistance which he
gave in my Latin exercises, to the arranging the
business of bringing out editions of my works.
He has always remained the same; and were I to
enumerate my friends, he would be placed by me
as the first on the list. When the traveller leaves
the mountains behind him, then for the first time
he sees them in their true form: so is it also with
friends.

I arrived at Paris by way of Cassel and the
Rhine. I retained a vivid impression of all that
I saw. The idea for a poem fixed itself firmer and
firmer in my mind; and I hoped, as it became more
clearly worked out, to propitiate my enemies by it.
There is an old Danish folk-song of Agnete and
the Merman, which bore an affinity to my own
state of mind, and to the treatment of which I felt
an inward impulse. The song tells that Agnete
wandered solitarily along the shore, when a merman rose up from the waves and decoyed her by
his speeches. She followed him to the bottom of

the sea, remained there seven years, and bore him
seven children. One day, as she sat by the
cradle, she heard the church bells sounding down
to her in the depths of the sea, and a longing seized
her heart to go to church. By her prayers and
tears she induced the merman to conduct her to
the upper world again, promising soon to return.
He prayed her not to forget his children, more
especially the little one in the cradle, stopped up
her ears and her mouth, and then led her upwards
to the sea-shore. When, however, she entered
the church, all the holy images, as soon as they
saw her, a daughter of sin and from the depths of
the sea, turned themselves round to the walls,
she was affrighted, and would not return although
the little ones in her home below were weeping.

I treated this subject freely, in a lyrical and
dramatic manner. I will venture to say that the
whole grew out of my heart; all the recollections
of our beechwoods and the open sea were blended
in it.

In the midst of the excitement of Paris I lived
in the spirit of the Danish folks-songs. The most
heartfelt gratitude to God filled my soul, because
I felt that all that I had, I had received through his

mercy; yet at the same time I took a lively interest in all that surrounded me. I was present at one of the July festivals, in their first freshness; it was in the year 1833. I saw the unveiling of Napoleon's pillar. I gazed on the world-experienced King Louis Philippe, who is evidently defended by providence. I saw the Duke of Orleans, full of health and the enjoyment of life, dancing at the gay people's ball, in the gay Maison de Ville. Accident led in Paris to my first meeting with Heine, the poet, who at that time occupied the throne in my poetical world. When I told him how happy this meeting and his kind words made me, he said that this could not very well be the case, else I should have sought him out. I replied, that I had not done so precisely because I estimated him so highly. I should have feared that he might have thought it ridiculous in me, an unknown Danish poet, to seek him out; "and," added I, "your sarcastic smile would deeply have wounded me." In reply, he said something friendly.

Several years afterwards, when we again met in Paris, he gave me a cordial reception, and I had a view into the brightly poetical portion of his soul.

Paul Düport met me with equal kindness. Victor Hugo also received me.

During my journey to Paris, and the whole month that I spent there, I heard not a single word from home. Could my friends perhaps have nothing agreeable to tell me? At length, however, a letter arrived; a large letter, which cost a large sum in postage. My heart beat with joy and yearning impatience; it was, indeed, my first letter. I opened it, but I discovered not a single written word, nothing but a Copenhagen newspaper, containing a lampoon upon me, and that was sent to me all that distance with postage unpaid, probably by the anonymous writer himself. This abominable malice wounded me deeply. I have never discovered who the author was; perhaps he was one of those who afterwards called me friend, and pressed my hand. Some men have base thoughts: I also have mine.

It is a weakness of my country-people, that commonly, when abroad, during their residence in large cities, they almost live exclusively in company together: they must dine together, meet at the theatre, and see all the lions of the place in company. Letters are read by each other; news of home is received and talked over, and at last they hardly know whether they are in a foreign land or their own. I had given way to the same weakness in Paris; and in leaving it, therefore, determined for one month to board myself in some quiet place in Switzerland, and live only among the French, so as to be compelled to speak their language, which was necessary to me in the highest degree.

In the little city of Locle, in a valley of the Jura mountains, where the snow fell in August, and the clouds floated below us, was I received by the amiable family of a wealthy watchmaker. They would not hear a word about payment. I lived among them and their friends as a relation, and when we parted the children wept. We had become friends, although I could not understand their patois: they shouted loudly into my ear, because they fancied I must be deaf, as I could not understand them. In the evenings, in that elevated region, there was a repose and a stillness in nature, and the sound of the evening bells ascended to us from the French frontier. At some distance from the city stood a solitary house, painted white and clean; on descending through two cellars, the

Two Drawings by Andersen

Above—"A Funeral Procession Passing My Window
in Rome, December 28, 1833."
Below—"My Bedroom in Villa Nuova"

Owned by the Andersen Museum in Odense

Two Drawings by Andersen

Above — "Interior: Reception Parlor, My Window in Rome, December 24, 1833"

Below — "My Bedroom in Villa Medici"

Owned by the Andersen Museum in Odense

noise of a millwheel was heard, and the rushing waters of a river which flowed on here, hidden from the world. I often visited this place in my solitary rambles, and here I finished my poem of "Agnete and the Merman," which I had begun in Paris.

I sent home this poem from Locle; and never, with my earlier or my later works, were my hopes so high as they were now. But it was received coldly. People said I had done it in imitation of Oehlenschläger, who at one time sent home masterpieces. Within the last few years, I fancy, this poem has been somewhat more read, and has met with its friends. It was, however, a step forwards, and it decided, as it were, unconsciously to me, my pure lyrical phasis. It has been also of late critically adjudged in Denmark, that, notwithstanding that on its first appearance it excited far less attention than some of my earlier and less successful works, still that in this the poetry is of a deeper, fuller, and more powerful character than anything which I had hitherto produced.

This poem closes one portion of my life.

CHAPTER V

On the 5th September, 1833, I crossed the Simplon on my way to Italy. On the very day, on which, fourteen years before, I had arrived poor and helpless in Copenhagen, did I set foot in this country of my longing and of my poetical happiness. It happened in this case, as it often does, by accident, without any arrangement on my part, as if I had preordained lucky days in the year; yet good fortune has so frequently been with me, that I perhaps only remind myself of its visits on my own self-elected days.

All was sunshine—all was spring! The vine hung in long trails from tree to tree; never since have I seen Italy so beautiful. I sailed on Lago Maggiore; ascended the cathedral of Milan; passed several days in Genoa, and made from thence a journey, rich in the beauties of nature, along the shore to Carrara. I had seen statues in Paris, but my eyes were closed to them; in Florence, before

the Venus de Medici, it was for the first time as if
scales fell from my eyes; a new world of art dis-
closed itself before me: that it was the first fruit
of my journey. Here it was that I first learned to
understand the beauty of form—the spirit, which
reveals itself in form. The life of the people—
nature—all was new to me; and yet as strangely
familiar as if I were come to a home where I had
lived in my childhood. With a peculiar rapidity
I seized upon everything, and entered into its life,
whilst a deep northern melancholy—it was not
home-sickness, but a heavy, unhappy feeling—
filled my breast. I received the news in Rome, of
how little the poem of Agnete, which I had sent
home, was thought of there; the next letter in
Rome, brought me the news that my mother was
dead. I was now quite alone in the world.

It was at this time, and in Rome, that my first
meeting with Hertz took place. In a letter which
I had received from Collin, he had said that it
would give him pleasure to hear that Hertz and I
had become friends; but even without this wish
it would have happened, for Hertz kindly offered
me his hand, and expressed sympathy with my
sorrow. He had, of all those with whom I was at

that time acquainted, the most variously cultivated mind. We had often disputations together,
even about the attacks which had been made upon
me at home as a poet. He, who had himself
given me a wound, said the following words, which
deeply impressed themselves on my memory:
" Your misfortune is, that you have been obliged
to print everything; the public has been able to
follow you step by step. I believe that even a
Goethe himself must have suffered the same fate,
had he been in your situation." And then he
praised my talent for seizing upon the characteristics of nature, and giving, by a few intuitive
sketches, pictures of familiar life. My intercourse
with him was very instructive to me, and I felt
that I had one merciful judge more. I travelled
in company with him to Naples, where we dwelt
together in one house.

In Rome I also became first acquainted with
Thorwaldsen. Many years before, when I had not
long been in Copenhagen, and was walking through
the streets as a poor boy, Thorwaldsen was there
too: that was on his first return home. We met
one another in the street. I knew that he was a
distinguished man in art; I looked at him, I

bowed; he went on, and then, suddenly turning round, came back to me and said, " Where have I seen you before? I think we know one another." I replied, " No, we do not know one another at all." I now related this story to him in Rome; he smiled, pressed my hand, and said, " Yet we felt at that time that we should become good friends." I read Agnete to him; and that which delighted me in his judgment upon it was the assertion, " It is just," said he, " as if I were walking at home in the woods, and heard the Danish lakes:" and then he kissed me.

One day, when he saw how distressed I was, and I related to him about the pasquinade which I had received from home in Paris, he gnashed his teeth violently, and said, in a momentary anger, " Yes, yes, I know the people; it would not have gone any better with me if I had remained there; I should then, perhaps, not even have obtained permission to set up a model. Thank God that I did not need them, for then they know how to torment and to annoy." He desired me to keep up a good heart, and then things could not fail of going well; and with that he told me of some dark passages in his own life, where he in like manner had been mortified and unjustly condemned.

After the Carnival, I left Rome for Naples; saw at Capri the blue Grotto, which was at that time first discovered; visited the temple at Pæstum, and returned in the Easter week to Rome, from whence I went through Florence and Venice to Vienna and Munich; but I had at that time neither time nor heart for Germany; and when I thought on Denmark, I felt fear and distress of mind about the bad reception which I expected to find there. Italy, with its scenery and its people's life, occupied my soul, and towards this land I felt a yearning. My earlier life, and what I had now seen, blended themselves together into an image—into poetry, which I was compelled to write down, although I was convinced that it would occasion me more trouble than joy, if my necessities at home should oblige me to print it. I had written already in Rome the first chapter. It was my novel of " The Improvisatore."

At one of my first visits to the theatre at Odense, as a little boy, where, as I have already mentioned, the representations were given in the German language, I saw the Donauweibchen, and the public applauded the actress of the principal part. Homage was paid to her, and she was honoured; and I vividly remember thinking how happy she must be. Many years afterwards, when as a student, I visited Odense, I saw, in one of the chambers of the hospital where the poor widows lived, and where one bed stood by another, a female portrait hanging over one bed in a gilt frame. It was Lessing's Emelia Galotti, and represented her as pulling the rose to pieces; but the picture was a portrait. It appeared singular in contrast with the poverty by which it was surrounded.

" Whom does it represent ? " asked I.

" Oh ! " said one of the old women, " it is the face of the German lady, the poor lady who once was an actress ! " And then I saw a little delicate woman, whose face was covered with wrinkles, and in an old silk gown that once had been black. That was the once celebrated singer, who, as the Donauweibchen, had been applauded by every one. This circumstance made an indelible impression upon me, and often occurred to my mind.

In Naples I heard Malibran for the first time.

Her singing and acting surpassed any thing which I had hitherto either heard or seen ; and yet I thought the while of the miserably poor singer in the hospital of Odense : the two figures blended into the Annunciata of the novel. Italy was the background for that which had been experienced and that which was imagined.

In August of 1834 I returned to Denmark. I wrote the first part of the book at Ingemann's, in Sorö, in a little chamber in the roof, among fragrant lime-trees. I finished it in Copenhagen.

At this time my best friends, even, had almost given me up as a poet ; they said that they had erred with regard to my talents. It was with difficulty that I found a publisher for the book. I received a miserable sum of money for it, and the "Improvisatore" made its appearance ; was read, sold out, and again published. The critics were silent ; the newspapers said nothing ; but I heard all around me of the interest which was felt for the work, and the delight that it occasioned. At length the poet Carl Bagger, who was at that time the editor of a newspaper, wrote the first critique upon it, and began ironically, with the customary tirade against me—" that it was all

over with this author, who had already passed
his heyday ; "—in short, he went the whole length
of the tobacco and tea criticism, in order suddenly
to dash out, and to express his extremely warm
enthusiasm for me ; and my book. People now
laughed at me, but I wept. This was my mood
of mind. I wept freely, and felt gratitude to God
and man.

" To the Conference Councillor Collin and to
his noble wife, in whom I found parents, whose
children were brethren and sisters to me, whose
house was my home, do I here present the best
of which I am possessed."—So ran the dedication.
Many who formerly had been my enemies, now
changed their opinion ; and among these one became my friend, who, I hope, will remain so through
the whole of my life. That was Hauch the poet,
one of the noblest characters with whom I am
acquainted. He had returned home from Italy
after a residence of years abroad, just at the time
when Heiberg's vaudevilles were intoxicating the
inhabitants of Copenhagen, and when my " Journey on Foot " was making me a little known. He
commenced a controversy with Heiberg, and somewhat scoffed at me. Nobody called his attention

to my better lyrical writings ; I was described to
to him as a spoiled, petulant child of fortune. He
now read my "Improvisatore," and feeling that
there was something good in me, his noble character
evinced itself by his writing a cordial letter to me,
in which he said, that he had done me an injustice,
and offered me now the hand of reconciliation.
From that time we became friends. He used
his influence for me with utmost zeal, and has
watched my onward career with heartfelt friendship. But so little able have so many people
been to understand what is excellent in him, or
the noble connection of heart between us two,
that not long since, when he wrote a novel, and
drew in it the caricature of a poet, whose vanity
ended in insanity, the people in Denmark, discovered that he had treated me with the greatest
injustice, because he had described in it my weakness. People must not believe that this was the
assertion of one single person, or a misapprehension
of my character ; no : and Hauch felt himself compelled to write a treatise upon me as a poet, that
he might show what a different place he assigned
to me.

But to return to the "Improvisatore." This

book raised my sunken fortunes ; collected my friends again around me, nay, even obtained for me new ones. For the first time I felt that I had obtained a due acknowledgment. The book was translated into German by Kruse, with a long title, " *Jugendleben und Träume eines italianischen Dichter's.*" I objected to the title ; but he declared that it was necessary in order to attract attention to the book.

Bagger had, as already stated, been the first to pass judgment on the work ; after an interval of some time a second critique made its appearance, more courteous, it is true, than I was accustomed to, but still passing lightly over the best things in the book, and dwelling on its deficiencies, and on the number of incorrectly written Italian words. And, as Nicolai's well-known book, "Italy as it really is," came out just then, people universally said, "Now we shall be able to see what it is about which Andersen has written, for from Nicolai a true idea of Italy may be obtained for the first time."

It was from Germany that resounded the first decided acknowledgment of the merits of my work, or rather perhaps its over estimation. I bow

myself in joyful gratitude, like a sick man toward
the sunshine, when my heart is grateful. I am
not, as the Danish Monthly Review, in its critique
of the "Improvisatore," condescended to assert,
an unthankful man, who exhibits in his work
a want of gratitude towards his benefactors. I
was indeed myself poor Antonio who sighed under
the burden which I had to bear,—*I*, the poor lad
who ate the bread of charity.   From Sweden also,
later, resounded my praise, and the Swedish newspapers contained articles in praise of this work,
which within the last two years has been equally
warmly received in England, where Mary Howitt,
the poetess, has translated it into English ; the
same good fortune also is said to have attended
the book in Holland and Russia. Every where
abroad resounded the loudest acknowledgment
of its excellence.

There exists in the public a power which is
stronger than all the critics and cliques. I felt
that I stood at home on firmer ground, and my
spirit again had moments in which it raised its
wings for flight. In this alteration of feeling
between gaiety and ill humour, I wrote my next
novel, " O.T.," which is regarded by many persons

in Denmark as my best work ;—an estimation
which I cannot myself award to it. It contains
characteristic features of town life. My first
Tales appeared before " O.T.; " but this is not
the place in which to speak of them. I felt just
at this time a strong mental impulse to write,
and I believed that I had found my true element
in novel-writing. In the following year, 1837,
I published " Only a Fiddler," a book which on
my part had been deeply pondered over, and the
details of which sprang fresh to the paper. My
design was to show that talent is not genius, and
that if the sunshine of good fortune be withheld,
this must go to the ground, though without losing
its nobler, better nature. This book likewise
had its partisans ; but still the critics would not
vouchsafe to me any encouragement ; they forgot
that with years the boy becomes a man, and
that people may acquire knowledge in other
than the ordinary ways. They could not separate
themselves from their old preconvinced opinions.
Whilst " O.T." was going through the press it
was submitted sheet by sheet to a professor of
the university, who had himself offered to undertake this work, and by two other able men also ;

notwithstanding all this, the Reviews said, "We
find the usual grammatical negligence, which we
always find in Andersen, in this work also." That
which contributed likewise to place this book in
the shade was the circumstance of Heiberg having
at that time published his Every-day Stories,
which were written in excellent language, and
with good taste and truth. Their own merits,
and the recommendation of their being Heiberg's,
who was the beaming star of literature, placed
them in the highest rank.

I had however advanced so far, that there no
longer existed any doubt as to my poetical ability,
which people had wholly denied to me before my
journey to Italy. Still not a single Danish critic
had spoken of the characteristics which are peculiar
to my novels. It was not until my works appeared
in Swedish that this was done, and then several
Swedish journals went profoundly into the subject
and analysed my works with good and honourable
intentions. The case was the same in Germany ;
and from this country too my heart was strengthened to proceed. It was not until last year that in
Denmark a man of influence, Hauch the poet,
spoke of the novels in his already mentioned

treatise, and with a few touches brought their characteristics prominently forward.

" The principal thing," says he, " in Andersen's best and most elaborate works, in those which are distinguished for the richest fancy, the deepest feeling, the most lively poetic spirit, is, of talent, or at least of a noble nature, which will struggle its way out of narrow and depressing circumstances. This is the case with his three novels, and with this purpose in view, it is really an important state of existence which he describes,—an inner world, which no one understands better than he, who has himself, drained out of the bitter cup of suffering and renunciation, painful and deep feelings which are closely related to those of his own experience, and from which Memory, who, according to the old significant myth, is the mother of the Muses, met him hand in hand with them. That which he, in these his works, relates to the world, deserves assuredly to be listened to with attention ; because, at the same time that it may be only the most secret inward life of the individual, yet it is also the common lot of men of talent and genius, at least when these are in needy circumstances. as in the case of those who are here placed before our eyes. In so far as in his 'Improvisatore,' in 'O.T.,' and in 'Only a Fiddler,' he represents not only himself, in his own separate individuality, but at the same time the momentous combat which so many have to pass through, and which he understands so well, because in it his own life has developed itself ; therefore in no instance can he be said to present to the reader what belongs to the world of illusion, but only that which bears witness to truth, and which, as is the case with all such testimony, has a universal and enduring worth.

"And still more than this, Andersen is not only the defender of talent and genius, but, at the same time, of every human heart which is unkindly and unjustly treated. And whilst he himself has so painfully suffered in that deep combat in which the Laocoon-snakes seize upon the outstretched hand ; whilst he himself has been compelled to drink from that wormwood-steeped bowl which the cold-blooded and arrogant world so constantly offers to those who are in depressed circumstances, he is fully capable of giving to his delineations in this respect a truth and an earnestness, nay, even a tragic and a pain-awakening

pathos that rarely fails of producing its effect
on the sympathising human heart. Who can read
that scene in his ' Only a Fiddler,' in which the
' highbred hound,' as the poet expresses it, turned
away with disgust from the broken victuals which
the poor youth received as alms, without recog-
nising, at the same time, that this is no game in
which vanity seeks for a triumph, but that it
expresses much more—human nature wounded
to its inmost depths, which here speaks out its
sufferings ? "

Thus is it spoken in Denmark of my works,
after an interval of nine or ten years ; thus speaks
the voice of a noble, venerated man. It is with
me and the critics as it is with wine,—the more
years pass before it is drunk the better is its
flavour.

During the year in which The Fiddler came out,
I visited for the first time the neighbouring country
of Sweden. I went by the Göta canal to Stockholm. At that time nobody understood what is
now called Scandinavian sympathies ; there still
existed a sort of mistrust inherited from the old
wars between the two neighbour nations. Little
was known of Swedish literature, and there were

only very few Danes who could easily read and
understand the Swedish language ; people scarcely
knew Tegnér's Frithiof and Axel, excepting
through translations. I had, however, read a
few other Swedish authors, and the deceased,
unfortunate Stagnelius pleased me more as a poet
than Tegnér, who represented poetry in Sweden.
I, who hitherto had only travelled into Germany
and southern countries, where by this means the
departure from Copenhagen was also the departure
from my mother tongue, felt, in this respect,
almost at home in Sweden : the languages are so
much akin, that of two persons each might read
in the language of his own country, and yet the
other understand him. It seemed to me, as a
Dane, that Denmark expanded itself ; kinship
with the people exhibited itself, in many ways,
more and more ; and I felt, livingly, how near akin
are Swedes, Danes, and Norwegians.

I met with cordial, kind people, and with these
I easily made acquaintance. I reckon this journey
among the happiest I ever made. I had no knowledge of the character of Swedish scenery, and
therefore I was in the highest degree astonished
by the Trollhätta-voyage, and by the extremely

picturesque situation of Stockholm. It sounds
to the uninitiated half like a fairy-tale, when one
says that the steam-boat goes up across the lakes
over the mountains, from whence may be seen
the outstretched pine and beechwoods below.
Immense sluices heave up and lower the vessel
again, whilst the travellers ramble through the
woods. None of the cascades of Switzerland,
none in Italy, not even that of Terni, have in them
any thing so imposing as that of Trollhätta. Such
is the impression, at all events, which it made on
me.

On this journey, and at this last mentioned
place, commenced a very interesting acquaintance,
and one which has not been without its influence
on me,—an acquaintance with the Swedish
authoress, Fredrika Bremer. I had just been
speaking with the Captain of the steam-boat
and some of the passengers about the Swedish
authors living in Stockholm, and I mentioned my
desire to see and converse with Miss Bremer.

" You will not meet with her," said the Captain,
" as she is at this moment on a visit in Norway."

" She will be coming back while I am there,"
said I in joke ; " I always am lucky in my journeys,

and that which I most wish for is always accomplished."

" Hardly this time, however," said the captain.

A few hours after this he came up to me laughing, with the list of the newly arrived passengers in his hand. " Lucky fellow," said he aloud, " you take good fortune with you ; Miss Bremer is here, and sails with us to Stockholm."

I received it as a joke ; he showed me the list, but still I was uncertain. Among the new arrivals, I could see no one who resembled an authoress. Evening came on, and about midnight we were on the great Wener lake. At sunrise I wished to have a view of this extensive lake, the shores of which could scarcely be seen ; and for this purpose I left the cabin. At the very moment that I did so, another passenger was also doing the same, a lady neither young nor old, wrapped in a shawl and cloak. I thought to myself, if Miss Bremer is on board, this must be she, and fell into discourse with her ; she replied politely, but still distantly, nor would she directly answer my question, whether she was the authoress of the celebrated novels. She asked after my name ; was acquainted with it, but confessed that she had read none of my works. She then inquired whether I had not some of them with me, and I lent her a copy of the " Improvisatore," which I had destined for Beskow. She vanished immediately with the volumes, and was not again visible all morning.

When I again saw her, her countenance was beaming, and she was full of cordiality ; she pressed my hand, and said that she had read the greater part of the first volume, and that she now knew me.

The vessel flew with us across the mountains, through quiet inland lakes and forests, till it arrived at the Baltic Sea, where islands lie scattered, as in the Archipelago, and where the most remarkable transition takes place from naked cliffs to grassy islands, and to those on which stand trees and houses. Eddies and breakers make it here necessary to take on board a skilful pilot ; and there are indeed some places where every passenger must sit quietly on his seat, whilst the eye of the pilot is riveted upon one point. On shipboard one feels the mighty power of nature, which at one moment seizes hold of the vessel and the next lets it go again.

Miss Bremer related many legends and many histories, which were connected with this or that island, or those farm-premises up aloft on the mainland.

In Stockholm, the acquaintance with her increased, and year after year the letters which have passed between us have strengthened it. She is a noble woman ; the great truths of religion, and the poetry which lies in the quiet circumstances of life, have penetrated her being.

It was not until after my visit to Stockholm that her Swedish translation of my novel came out ; my lyrical poems only, and my Journey on Foot, were known to a few authors ; these received me with the utmost kindness, and the lately deceased Dahlgrén, well known by his humorous poems, wrote a song in my honour— in short, I met with hospitality, and countenances beaming with Sunday gladness. Sweden and its inhabitants became dear to me. The city itself, by its situation and its whole picturesque appearance, seemed to me to emulate Naples. Of course, this last has the advantage of fine atmosphere, and the sunshine of the south ; but the view of Stockholm is just as imposing ; it has also some resemblance to Constantinople, as from Pera, only that the minarets are wanting. There prevails a great variety of colouring in the capital of Sweden ; white painted buildings ; frame-work houses, with the wood painted red ; barracks of turf, with flowering plants ; fir trees and birches look out from among the houses, and the churches with their balls and towers. The streets in Södermalm ascend by flights of wooden steps up from the Mälar lake, which is all active with smoking steam-vessels, and with boats rowed by women in gay-coloured dresses.

I had brought with me a letter of introduction from Oersted, to the celebrated Berzelius, who gave me a good reception in the old city of Upsala. From this place I returned to Stockholm. City, country, and people, were all dear to me ; it seemed to me, as I said before, that the boundaries of my native land had stretched themselves out, and I now first felt the kindredship of the three peoples, and in this feeling I wrote a Scandinavian song, a hymn of praise for all the three nations, for that which was peculiar and best in each one of them.

" One can see that the Swedes made a deal of him," was the first remark which I heard at home on this song.

Years pass on ; the neighbours understand each other better; Oehlenschläger, Fredrika Bremer, and Tegnér, cause them mutually to read each other's authors, and the foolish remains of the old enmity, which had no other foundation than that they did not know each other, vanished. There now prevails a beautiful, cordial relationship between Sweden and Denmark. A Scandinavian club has been established in Stockholm ; and with this my song came to honour ; and it was then said, "it will outlive everything that Andersen has written : " which was as unjust as when they said that it was only the product of flattered vanity. This song is now sung in Sweden as well as in Denmark.

On my return home I began to study history industriously, and made myself still further acquainted with the literature of foreign countries. Yet still the volume which afforded me the greatest pleasure was that of nature ; and during a summer residence among the country seats of Funen, and more especially at Lykkesholm, with its highly romantic site in the midst of woods, and at the noble seat of Glorup, from whose possessor I met with the most friendly reception, did I acquire

more true wisdom, assuredly, in my solitary
rambles, than I ever could have gained from the
schools.

The house of the Conference Councillor Collin
in Copenhagen was at that time, as it has been
since, a second father's house to me, and there
I had parents, and brothers and sisters. The
best circles of social life were open to me, and the
student life interested me : here I mixed in the
pleasures of youth. The student life of Copenhagen is, besides this, different from that of the
German cities, and was at this time peculiar and
full of life. For me this was most perceptible
in the student's clubs, where students and professors were accustomed to meet each other : there
was there no boundary drawn between the youthful
and elder men of letters. In this club were to
be found the journals and books of various countries ; once a week an author would read his last
work; a concert or some peculiar burlesque enter-
tainment would take place. It was here that what
may be called the first Danish people's comedies
took their origin,—comedies in which the events
of the day were worked up always in an innocent,
but witty and amusing manner. Sometimes

dramatic representations were given in the presence of ladies for the furtherance of some noble purpose, as lately to assist Thorwaldsen's Museum, to raise funds for the execution of Bissen's statue in marble, and for similar ends. The professors and students were the actors. I also appeared several times as an actor, and convinced myself that my terror at appearing on the stage was greater than the talent which I perhaps possessed. Besides this, I wrote and arranged several pieces, and thus gave my assistance. Several scenes from this time, the scenes in the student's club, I have worked up in my romance of "O. T." The humour and love of life observable in various passages of this book, and in the little dramatic pieces written about his time, are owing to the influence of the family of Collin, where much good was done me in that respect, so that my morbid turn of mind was unable to gain the mastery of me. Collin's eldest married daughter, especially, exercised great influence over me, by her merry humour and wit. When the mind is yielding and elastic, like the expanse of ocean, it readily, like the ocean, mirrors its environments.

My writings, in my own country, were now

classed among those which were always bought
and read : therefore for each fresh work I received
a higher payment. Yet, truly, when you consider
what a circumscribed world the Danish reading
world is, you will see that this payment could not
be the most liberal. Yet I had to live. Collin,
who is one of the men who do more than they
promise, was my help, my consolation, my support.

At this time the late Count Conrad von Rantzau-
Breitenburg, a native of Holstein, was Prime
Minister in Denmark. He was of a noble, amiable
nature, a highly educated man, and possessed of a
truly chivalrous disposition. He carefully observed the movements in German and Danish
literature. In his youth he had travelled much,
and spent a long time in Spain and Italy. He
read my Improvisatore in the original ; his imagination was powerfully seized by it, and he spoke both
at Court and in his own private circles of my book
in the warmest manner. He did not stop here ;
he sought me out, and became my benefactor and
friend. One forenoon, whilst I was sitting solitarily in my little chamber, this friendly man stood
before me for the first time. He belonged to that
class of men who immediately inspire you with

confidence ; he besought me to visit him, and frankly asked me whether there were no means by which he could be of use to me. I hinted how oppressive it was to be *forced* to write in order to live, always to be forced to think of the morrow, and not move free from care, to be able to develope your mind and thoughts. He pressed my hand in a friendly manner, and promised to be an efficient friend. Collin and Oersteed secretly associated themselves with him, and became my intercessors.

Already for many years there had existed, under Frederick VI., an institution which does the highest honour to the Danish government, namely, that beside the considerable sum expended yearly, for the travelling expenses of young literary men and artists, a small pension shall be awarded to such of them as enjoy no office emoluments. All our most important poets have had a share of this assistance,—Oehlenschläger, Ingemann, Heiberg, C. Winther, and others. Hertz had just then received such a pension, and his future life was made thus the more secure. It was my hope and my wish that the same good fortune might be mine—and it was. Frederick VI. granted me two hundred rix-dollars banco yearly. I was filled with gratitude and joy. I was no longer *forced* to write in order to live ; I had a sure support in the possible event of sickness ; I was less dependent upon the people about me. A new chapter of my life began.

CHAPTER VI

FROM this day forward, it was as if a more constant sunshine had entered my heart. I felt within myself more repose, more certainty ; it was clear to me, as I glanced back over my earlier life, that a loving Providence watched over me, that all was directed for me by a higher power ; and the firmer becomes such a conviction, the more secure does a man feel himself. My childhood lay behind me, my youthful life began properly from this period ; hitherto it had been only an arduous swimming against the stream. The spring of my life commenced ; but still the spring had its dark days, its storms, before it advanced to settled summer ; it has these in order to develope what shall then ripen.

That which one of my dearest friends wrote to me on one of my later travels abroad, may serve as an introduction to what I have here to relate. He wrote in his own peculiar style :—" It is your vivid imagination which creates the idea of your being despised in Denmark ; it is utterly untrue. You and Denmark agree admirably, and you would agree still better, if there were in Denmark no theatre—*Hinc illæ lacrymæ* ! This cursed theatre. Is this, then, Denmark? and are you, then, nothing but a writer for the theatre ? "

Herein lies a solid truth. The theatre has been the cave out of which most of the evil storms have burst upon me. They are peculiar people, these people of the theatre,—as different, in fact, from others, as Bedouins from Germans ; from the first pantomimist to the first lover, every one places himself systematically in one scale, and puts all the world in the other. The Danish theatre is a good theatre, it may indeed be placed on a level with the Burg theatre in Vienna ; but the theatre in Copenhagen plays too great a part in conversation, and possesses in most circles too much importance. I am not sufficiently acquainted with the stage and the actors in other great cities, and therefore cannot compare them with our theatre ; but ours has too little military discipline, and this is absolutely necessary where many people have to form a whole, even when that whole is an artistical one. The most distinguished dramatic poets in Denmark—that is to say, in Copenhagen, for there only is a theatre—have their troubles. Those actors and actresses who, through talent or the popular favour, take the first rank, very often place themselves above both the managers and authors. These must pay court to them, or they may ruin a part, or what is still worse, may spread abroad an unfavourable opinion of the piece previous to its being acted ; and thus you have a coffee-house criticism before anyone ought properly to know anything of the work. It is moreover characteristic of the people of Copenhagen, that when a new piece is announced, they do not say, " I am glad of it," but, " It will probably be good for nothing ; it will be hissed off the stage." That hissing-off plays a great part, and is an amusement which fills the house ; but it is not the bad actor who is hissed, no, the author and the composer only are the criminals ; for them the scaffold is erected. Five minutes is the usual time, and the whistles resound, and the lovely women smile and felicitate themselves, like the Spanish ladies at their bloody bullfights. All our most eminent dramatic writers have been whistled down,—as

Oehlenschläger, Heiberg, Overskou, and others ; to say nothing of foreign classics, as Molière. In the mean time the theatre is the most profitable sphere of labour for the Danish writer, whose public does not extend far beyond the frontiers. This had induced me to write the opera-text already spoken of, on account of which I was so severely criticised ; and an internal impulse drove me afterwards to add some other works. Collin was no longer manager of the theatre, Counsellor of Justice Molbech had taken his place ; and the tyranny which now commenced degenerated into the comic. I fancy that in course of time the manuscript volumes of the censorship, which are preserved in the theatre, and in which Molbech has certainly recorded his judgments on received and rejected pieces, will present some remarkable characteristics. Over all that I wrote the staff was broken ! One way was open to me by which to bring my pieces on the stage ; and that was to give them to those actors who in summer gave representations at their own cost. In the summer of 1839 I wrote the vaudeville of " The Invisible One on Sprogö," to scenery which had been painted for another piece which fell through ; and the unrestrained merriment of the piece gave it such favour with the public, that I obtained its acceptance by the manager ; and that light sketch still maintains itself on the boards, and has survived such a number of representations as I had never anticipated.

This approbation, however, procured me no further advantage, for each of my succeeding dramatic works, received only rejection, and occasioned me only mortification. Nevertheless, seized by the idea and the circumstances of the little French narrative, " *Les épaves*," I determined to dramatise it ; and as I had often heard that I did not possess the assiduity sufficient to work my material well, I resolved to labour this drama— " The Mulatto "—from the beginning to the end, in the most diligent manner, and to compare it in alternately rhyming verse, as was then the fashion. It was a foreign subject of which I availed myself ; but if verses are music, I at least endeavoured to adapt my music to the text, and to let the poetry of another diffuse itself through my spiritual blood ; so that people should not be heard to say, as they had done before, regarding the romance of Walter Scott, that composition was cut down and fitted to the stage.

The piece was ready, and declared by able men, old friends, and actors who were to appear in it, to be excellent ; a rich dramatic capacity lay in the material, and my lyrical composition clothed this with so fresh a green, that people appeared satisfied. The piece was sent in, and was rejected by Molbech. It was sufficiently known that what he cherished for the boards, withered there the first evening ; but that what he cast away as weeds were flowers for the garden—a real consolation for me. The assistant-manager, Privy Counsellor of State Adler, a man of taste and liberality, became the patron of my work ; and since a very favourable opinion of it already prevailed with the public, after I had read it to many persons, it was resolved on for representation. I had the honour to read it before my present King and Queen, who received me in a very kind and friendly manner, and from whom, since that time, I have experienced many proofs of favour and cordiality. The day of representation arrived ; the bills were posted ; I had not closed my eyes through the whole night from excitement and expectation ;

the people already stood in throngs before the theatre, to procure tickets, when royal messengers galloped through the streets, solemn groups collected, the minute guns pealed—Frederick VI. had died that morning!

For two months more was the theatre closed, and was opened under Christian VIII., with my drama—" The Mulatto ; " which was received with the most triumphant acclamation ; but I could not at once feel the joy of it, I felt only relieved from a state of excitement, and breathed more freely.

This piece continued through a series of representations to receive the same approbation ; many placed this work far above all my former ones, and considered that with it began my proper poetical career. It was soon translated into the Swedish, and acted with applause at the royal theatre in Stockholm. Travelling players introduced it into the smaller towns in the neighbouring country ; a Danish company gave it in the original language, in the Swedish city Malmö, and a troop of students from the university town of Lund, welcomed it with enthusiasm. I had been for a week previous on a visit at some Swedish country houses, where I was entertained with so much cordial kindness that the recollection will never quit my bosom ; and there, in a foreign country, I received the first public testimony of honour, and which has left upon me the deepest and most inextinguishable impression. I was invited by some students of Lund to visit their ancient town. Here a public dinner was given to me ; speeches were made, toasts were pronounced ; and as I was in the evening in a family circle, I was informed that the students meant to honour me with a serenade.

I felt myself actually overcome by this intelligence ; my heart throbbed feverishly as I descried the thronging troop, with their blue caps, and arm-in-arm approaching the house. I experienced a feeling of humiliation ; a most lively consciousness of my deficiencies, so that I seemed bowed to the very earth at the moment others were elevating me. As they all uncovered their heads while I stepped forth, I had need of all my thoughts to avoid bursting into tears. In the feeling that I was unworthy of all this, I glanced round to see whether a smile did not pass over the face of some one, but I could discern nothing of the kind ;

and such a discovery would, at that moment, have inflicted on me the deepest wound.

After an hurrah, a speech was delivered, of which I clearly recollect the following words :— " When your native land and the natives of Europe offer you their homage, then may you never forget that the first public honours were conferred on you by the students of Lund."

When the heart is warm, the strength of the expression is not weighed. I felt it deeply, and replied, that from this moment I became aware that I must assert a name in order to render myself worthy of these tokens of honour. I pressed the hands of those nearest to me, and returned them thanks so deep, so heartfelt,— certainly never was an expression of thanks more sincere. When I returned to my chamber, I went aside, in order to weep out this excitement, this overwhelming sensation. " Think no more of it, be joyous with us," said some of my lively Swedish friends ; but a deep earnestness had entered my soul. Often has the memory of this time come back to me ; and no noble-minded man, who reads these pages, will discover a vanity in the fact, that I have lingered so long over this moment of life, which scorched the roots of pride rather than nourished them.

My drama was now to be brought on the stage at Malmö ; the students wished to see it ; but I hastened my departure, that I might not be in the theatre at the time. With gratitude and joy fly my thoughts towards the Swedish University city, but I myself have not been there again since. In the Swedish newspapers the honours paid me were mentioned, and it was added that the Swedes were not unaware that in my own country there was a clique which persecuted me ; but that this should not hinder my neighbours from offering me the honours which they deemed my due.

It was when I had returned to Copenhagen that I first truly felt how cordially I had been received by the Swedes : amongst some of my old and tried friends I found the most genuine sympathy. I saw tears in their eyes, tears of joy for the honours paid me ; and especially, said they, for the manner in which I had received them. There is but one manner for me ; at once, in the midst of joy, I fly with thanks to God.

There were certain persons who smiled at the enthusiasm ; certain voices raised themselves already against " The Mulatto ; "—" the material was merely borrowed ; " the French narrative was scrupulously studied. That exaggerated praise which I had received, now made me sensitive to the blame ; I could bear it less easily than before, and saw more clearly, that it did not spring out of interest in the matter, but it was only uttered in order to mortify me. For the rest, my mind was fresh and elastic ; I conceived precisely at this time the idea of " The Picture-Book without Pictures," and worked it out. This little book appears, to judge by the reviews and the number of editions, to have obtained an extraordinary popularity in Germany ; it was also translated into Swedish, and dedicated to myself ; at home, it was less esteemed ; people talked only of The Mulatto ; and finally, only of the borrowed material of it. I determined, therefore, to produce a new dramatic work, in which both subject and development, in fact, everything should be of my conception. I had the idea, and now wrote the tragedy of The Moorish Maiden, hoping through this to stop the mouths of my detractors, and to assert my place as a dramatic poet. I hoped, too, through the income from this, together with the proceeds of The Mulatto, to be able to make a fresh journey, not only to Italy, but to Greece and Turkey. My first going abroad had more than all besides operated towards my intellectual development; I was therefore full of the passion for travel, and of the endeavour to acquire more knowledge of nature and of human life.

My new piece did not please Heiberg, nor indeed my dramatic endeavours at all; his wife—for whom the chief part appeared to me especially to be written—refused, and that not in the most friendly manner, to play it. Deeply wounded, I went forth. I lamented this to some individuals. Whether this was repeated, or whether a complaint against the favourite of the public is a crime,— enough: from this hour Heiberg became my opponent, —he whose intellectual rank I so highly estimated,—he with whom I would so willingly have allied myself,—and he who so often—I will venture to say it—I had approached with the whole sincerity of my nature. I have constantly declared his wife to be so distinguished an actress, and continue still so entirely of this opinion, that I would not hesitate one moment to assert that she would have a European reputation, were the

Danish language as widely diffused as the German or the French. In tragedy she is, by the spirit and the geniality with which she comprehends and fills any part, a most interesting object ; and in comedy she stands unrivalled.

The wrong may be on my side or not,—no matter : a party was opposed to me. I felt myself wounded, excited by many coincident annoyances there. I felt uncomfortable in my native country, yes, almost ill. I therefore left my piece to its fate, and suffering and disconcerted, I hastened forth. In this mood, I wrote a prologue to The Moorish Maiden ; which betrayed my irritated mind far too palpably. If I would represent this portion of my life more clearly and reflectively, it would require me to penetrate into the mysteries of the theatre, to analyse our æsthetic cliques, and to drag into conspicuous notice many individuals, who do not belong to publicity. Many persons in my place would, like me, have fallen ill, or would have resented it vehemently : perhaps the latter would have been the most sensible.

At my departure, many of my young friends amongst the students prepared a banquet for me ; and amongst the elder ones who were present to receive me were Collin, Oehlenschläger and Oersted. This was somewhat of sunshine in the midst of my mortification; songs by Oehlenschläger and Hillerup were sung; and I found cordiality and friendship, as I quitted my country in distress. This was in October of 1840.

For the second time I went to Italy and Rome, to Greece and Constantinople—a journey which I have described after my own manner in A Poet's Bazaar.

In Holstein I continued some days with Count Rantzau-Breitenburg, who had before invited me, and whose ancestral castle I now for the first time visited. Here I became acquainted with the rich scenery of Holstein, heath and moorland, and then hastened by Nuremberg to Munich, where I again met with Cornelius and Schelling, and was kindly received by Kaulbach and Schelling. I cast a passing glance on the artistic life in Munich, but for the most part pursued my own solitary course, sometimes filled with the joy of life, but often despairing of my powers. I possessed a peculiar talent, that of lingering on the gloomy side of life, of extracting the bitter from it, of tasting it; and understood well, when the whole was exhausted, how to torment myself.

In the winter season I crossed the Brenner, remained some days in Florence, which I had before visited for a longer time, and about Christmas reached Rome. Here again I saw the noble treasures of art, met old friends, and once more passed a Carnival and Moccoli. But not alone was I bodily ill ; nature around me appeared likewise to sicken ; there was neither the tranquillity nor the freshness which attended my first sojourn in Rome. The rocks quaked, the Tiber twice rose into the streets, fever raged, and snatched numbers away. In a few days Prince Borghese lost his wife and three sons. Rain and wind prevailed ; in short it was dismal, and from home cold lotions were sent me. My letters told me that The Moorish Maiden had several times been acted through, and had gone quietly off the stage ; but, as was seen beforehand, a small public only had been present, and therefore the manager had laid the piece aside. Other Copenhagen letters to our countrymen in Rome spoke with enthusiasm of a new work by Heiberg ; a satirical poem—A Soul after Death. It was but just out, they wrote ; all Copenhagen was full of it, and Andersen was famously handled in it.

The book was admirable, and I was made ridiculous in it. That was the whole which I heard,—all that I knew. No one told me what really was said of me ; wherein lay the amusement and the ludicrous. It is doubly painful to be ridiculed when we don't know wherefore we are so. The information operated like molten lead dropped into a wound, and agonised me cruelly. It was not till after my return to Denmark that I read this book, and found that what was said of me in it, was really nothing in itself which was worth laying to heart. It was a jest over my celebrity " from Schonen to Hundsrück," which did not please Heiberg ; he therefore sent my Mulatto and the Moorish Maiden to the infernal regions, where—and that was the most witty conceit—the condemned were doomed to witness the performance of both pieces in one evening ; and then they could go away and lay themselves down quietly. I found the poetry, for the rest, so excellent, that I was half induced to write to Heiberg, and to return him my thanks for it ; but I slept upon this fancy, and when I awoke and was more composed, I feared lest such thanks should be misunderstood; and so gave it up.

In Rome, as I have said, I did not see the book; I only heard the arrows whizz and felt their wound, but I did not know what the poison was which lay concealed in them. It seemed to me that Rome was no joy-bringing city; when I was there before, I had also passed dark and bitter days. I was ill, for the first time in my life, truly and bodily ill, and I made haste to get away.

The Danish poet Holst was then in Rome; he had recieved this year a travelling pension. Holst had written an elegy on King Frederick VI., which went from mouth to mouth, and awoke an enthusiasm, like that of Becker's contemporaneous Rhine song in Germany. He had lived in the same house with me in Rome, and showed me much sympathy; with him I made the journey to Naples, where, notwithstanding it was March, the sun would not properly shine, and the snow lay on the hills around. There was fever in my blood; I suffered in body and in mind; and I soon lay so severely affected by it, that certainly nothing but a speedy blood-letting, to which my excellent Neapolitan landlord compelled me, saved my life.

In a few days I grew sensibly better; and I now proceeded by a French war steamer to Greece. Holst accompanied me on board. It was now as if a new life had arisen for me; and in truth this was the case: and if this does not appear legibly in my later writings, yet it manifested itself in my views of life, and in my whole inner development. As I saw my European home lie far behind me, it seemed to me as if a stream of forgetfulness flowed of all bitter and rankling remembrances: I felt health in my blood, health in my thoughts, and freshly and courageously I again raised my head.

Like another Switzerland, with a loftier and clearer heaven than the Italian, Greece lay before me; nature made a deep and solemn impression upon me; I felt the sentiment of standing on the great battlefield of the world, where nation had striven with nation, and had persisted. No single poem can embrace such greatness; every scorched-up bed of a stream, every height, every stone, has mighty memoirs to relate. How little appear the inequalities of daily life in such a place! A kingdom of ideas streamed through me, and with such a fulness, that none of them fixed themselves on paper. I had a desire to express the idea, that the godlike was here on earth to maintain its contest, that it is thrust backward, and yet advances again victoriously through all ages; and I found in the legend of the Wandering Jew an occasion for it. For twelve months this Fiction had been emerging from the sea of my thoughts; often did it wholly fill me; sometimes I fancied with the alchemists that I had dug up the treasure; then again it sunk suddenly, and I despaired of ever being able to bring it to the light. I felt what a mass of knowledge of various kinds I must first acquire. Often at home, when I was compelled to hear reproofs on what they call a want of study, I had sate deep into the night, and had studied history in Hegel's Philosophy of History. I said nothing of this, or other studies would immediately have been spoken of, in the manner of an instructive lady, who said, that people justly complained that I did not possess learning enough. "You have really no mythology," said she; "in all your poems there appears no single God. You must pursue mythology; you must read Racine and

HANS CHRISTIAN ANDERSEN
From a Painting by C. A. Jensen, about 1838

Corneille." That she called learning; and in like manner every one had something peculiar to recommend. For my poem of Ahasuerus I had read much and noted much, but yet not enough; in Greece, I thought, the whole will collect itself into clearness. The poem is not yet ready, but I hope that it will become so to my honour; for it happens with the children of the spirit, as with the earthly ones,—they grow as they sleep.

In Athens I was heartily welcomed by Professor Ross, a native of Holstein, and by my countrymen. I found hospitality and a friendly feeling in the noble Prokesch-Osten; even the King and Queen received me most graciously. I celebrated my birthday in the Acropolis.

From Athens I sailed to Smyrna, and with me it was no childish pleasure to be able to tread another quarter of the globe. I felt a devotion in it, like that which I felt as a child when I entered the old church at Odense. I thought on Christ, who bled on this earth; I thought on Homer, whose song eternally resounds hence over the earth. The shores of Asia preached to me their sermons, and were perhaps more impressive than any sermon in any church can be.

In Constantinople I passed eleven interesting days ; and according to my good fortune in travel, the birthday of Mahomet itself fell exactly during my stay there. I saw the grand illumination which completely transported me into the Thousand and One Nights.

Our Danish ambassador lived several miles from Constantinople, and I had therefore no opportunity of seeing him ; but I found a cordial reception with the Austrian internuntius, Baron von Stürmer. With him I had a German home and friends. I contemplated making my return by the Black Sea and up the Danube ; but the country was disturbed ; it was said there had been several thousand Christians murdered. My companions of the voyage, in the hotel where I resided, gave up this route of the Danube, for which I had the greatest desire, and collectively counselled me against it. But in this case I must return again by Greece and Italy—it was a severe conflict.

I do not belong to the courageous ; I feel fear, especially in little dangers ; but in great ones, and when an advantage is to be won, then I have a will, and it has grown firmer with years. I may tremble, I may fear ; but I still do that which I consider the most proper to be done. I am not ashamed to confess my weakness ; I hold that when out of my own true conviction we run counter to our inborn fear, we have done our duty. I had a strong desire to become acquainted with the interior of the country, and to traverse the Danube in its greatest expansion. I battled with myself ; my imagination pointed to me the most horrible circumstances ; it was an anxious night. In the morning, I took counsel with Baron Stürmer ; and as he was of opinion that I might undertake the voyage, I determined upon it. From the moment I had taken my determination I had the most immovable reliance on Providence, and flung myself calmly on my fate. Nothing happened to me. The voyage was prosperous, and after the quarantine on the Wallachian frontier, which was painful enough to me, I arrived in Vienna on the twenty-first day of the journey. The sight of its towers, and the meeting with numerous Danes, awoke in me the thought of being speedily again at home. The idea bowed down my heart and sad recollections and mortifications rose up, within me once more.

In August, 1841, I was again in Copenhagen

There I wrote my recollections of travel, under the title of A Poet's Bazaar, in several chapters, according to the countries. In various places abroad I had met with individuals, as at home, to whom I felt myself attached. A poet is like the bird ; he gives what he has, and he gives a song. I was desirous to give every one of those dear ones such a song. It was a fugitive idea, born, may I venture to say, in a grateful mood. Count Rantzau-Breitenburg, who had resided in Italy, who loved the land, and was become a friend and benefactor to me through my Improvisatore, must love that part of the book which treated of his country. To Liszt and Thalberg, who had both shown me the greatest friendship, I dedicated the portion which contained the voyage up the Danube, because one was a Hungarian and the other an Austrian. With these indications, the reader will easily be able to trace out the thought which influenced me in the choice of each dedication. But these appropriations were, in my native country, regarded as a fresh proof of my vanity :— " I wished to figure with great names, to name distinguished people as my friends."

The book has been translated into several

languages, and the dedications with it. I know not how they have been regarded abroad; if I have been judged there as in Denmark, I hope that this explanation will change the opinion concerning them. In Denmark my Bazaar procured me the most handsome remuneration that I have as yet received,—a proof that I was at length read there. No regular criticism appeared upon it, if we except notices in some daily papers, and afterwards in the poetical attempt of a young writer, who, a year before, had testified to me in writing his love, and his wish to do me honour; but who now, in his first public appearance, launched his satirical poem against his friend. I was personally attached to this young man, and am so still. He assuredly thought more on the popularity he would gain by sailing in the wake of Heiberg, than on the pain he would inflict on me.

The newspaper criticism in Copenhagen was infinitely stupid. It was set down as exaggerated, that I could have seen the whole round blue globe of the moon in Smyrna at the time of the new moon. That was called fancy and extravagance, which there every one sees who can open his eyes. The new moon has a dark blue and perfectly round disc.

The Danish critics have generally no open eye for nature : even the highest and most cultivated monthly periodical of literature in Denmark censured me once because in a poem I had described a rainbow by moonlight. That too was my fancy, which, said they, carried me too far. When I said in the Bazaar, " if I were a painter, I would paint this bridge ; but, as I am no painter, but a poet, I must therefore speak," etc. Upon this the critic says, " He is so vain, that he tells us himself that he is a poet." There is something so pitiful in such criticism, that one cannot be wounded by it ; but even when we are the most peaceable of men, we feel a desire to flagellate such wet dogs, who come into our rooms and lay themselves down in the best place in them. There might be a whole Fool's Chronicle written of all the absurd and shameless things which, from my first appearance before the public till this moment, I have been compelled to hear.

In the meantime the Bazaar was much read, and made what is called a hit. I received, connected with this book, much encouragement and many recognitions from individuals of the highest distinction in the realms of intellect in my native land.

The journey had strengthened me both in mind and body ; I began to show indications of a firmer purpose, a more certain judgment. I was now in harmony with myself and with mankind around me.

Political life in Denmark had, at that time, arrived at a higher development, producing both good and evil fruits. The eloquence which had formerly accustomed itself to the Demosthenic mode, that of putting little pebbles in the mouth, the little pebbles of every day life, now exercised itself more freely on subjects of greater interest. I felt no call thereto, and no necessity to mix myself up in such matters ; for I then believed that the politics of our times were a great misfortune to many a poet. Madame Politics is like Venus : they whom she decoys into her castle perish. It fares with the writings of these poets as with the newspapers : they are seized upon, read, praised, and forgotten. In our days every one wishes to rule ; the subjective makes its power of value ; people forget that that which is thought of cannot always be carried out, and that many things look very different when contemplated from the top of the tree, to what they did when seen from its roots. I will bow myself before him who is influenced by a noble conviction, and who only desires that which is conducive to good, be he prince or man of the people. Politics are no affair of mine. God has imparted to me another mission : that I felt, and that I feel still.

I met in the so-called first families of the country a number of friendly, kind-hearted men, who valued the good that was in me, received me into their circles, and permitted me to participate in the happiness of their opulent summer residences ; so that, still feeling independent, I could thoroughly give myself up to the pleasures of nature, the solitude of woods, and country life. There for the first time I lived wholly among the scenery of Denmark, and there I wrote the greater number of my fairy tales. On the banks of quiet lakes, amid the woods, on the green grassy pastures, where the game sprang past me and the stork paced along on his red legs, I heard nothing of politics, nothing of polemics ; I heard no one practising himself in Hegel's phraseology. Nature, which was around me and within me, preached to me of my calling. I spent many happy days at the old home of Gisselfeld, formerly a monastery, which stands in the deepest solitude of the woods, surrounded with lakes and hills. The possessor of this fine place, the old Countess Danneskjold, mother of the Duchess of Augustenburg, was an agreeable and excellent lady. I was there not as a poor child of the people, but as a cordially-received guest. The beeches now overshadow her grave in the midst of that pleasant scenery to which her heart was allied.

Close by Gisselfeld, but in a still finer situation, and of much greater extent, lies the estate of Bregentved, which belongs to Count Moltke, Danish Minister of Finance. The hospitality which I met with in this place, one of the richest and most beautiful of our country, and the happy, social life which surrounded me here, have diffused a sunshine over my life.

It may appear, perhaps, as if I desired to bring the names of great people prominently forward, and to make a parade of them ; or as if I wished in this way to offer a kind of thanks to my bene-factors. They need it not, and I should be obliged to mention many other names still if this were my intention. I speak, however, only of these two places, and of Nysö, which belongs to Baron Stampe, and which has become celebrated through Thorwaldsen. Here I lived much with the great sculptor, and here I became acquainted with one of my dearest young friends, the future possessor of the place.

Knowledge of life in these various circles had had great influence on me : among princes, among the nobility, and among the poorest of the people, I have met with specimens of noble humanity. We all of us resemble each other in that which is good and best.

Winter life in Denmark has likewise its attractions and its rich variety. I spent also some time in the country during this season, and made myself acquainted with its peculiar characteristics. The greatest part of my time, however, I passed in Copenhagen. I felt myself at home with the married sons and daughters of Collin, where a number of amiable children were growing up. Every year strengthened the bond of friendship between myself and the nobly-gifted composer Hartmann : art and the freshness of nature prospered in his house. Collin was my counsellor in practical life, and Oersted in my literary affairs. The theatre, was, if I may so say, my club. I visited it every evening, and in this very year I had received a place in the so-called Court stalls. An author must, as a matter of course, work himself up to it. After the first accepted piece he obtains admission to the pit ; after the second greater work, in the stalls, where the actors have their seats ; and after three larger works, or a succession of lesser pieces, the poet is advanced to the best places. Here were to be found Thorwaldsen, Oehlenschläger, and several older poets ; and here also, in 1840, I obtained a place, after I had given in seven pieces. Whilst Thorwaldsen lived, I often, by his own wish, sate at his side. Oehlenschläger was also my neighbour, and in many an evening hour, when no one dreamed of it, my soul was steeped in deep humility, as I sate between these great spirits. The different periods of my life passed before me ; the time when I sate on the hindmost bench in the box of the female figurantes, as well as that in which, full of childish superstition, I knelt down there upon the stage and repeated the Lord's Prayer, just before the very place where I now sate among the first and the most distinguished men. At the time, perhaps, when a countryman of mine thus thought of and passed a judgment upon me,— " there he sits, between the two great spirits, full of arrogance and pride ; " he may now perceive by this acknowledgement how unjustly he has judged me. Humility, and prayer to God for strength to deserve my happiness, filled my heart. May he always enable me to preserve these feelings ! I enjoyed the friendship of Thorwaldsen as well as of Oehlenschläger, those two most distinguished stars in the horizon of the North. I may here bring forward their reflected glory in and around me.

There in the character of Oehlenschläger, when he is not seen in the circle of the great, where he is quiet and reserved, something so open and child-like, that no one can help becoming attached to him. As a poet, he holds in the North a position of as great importance as Göethe did in Germany. He is in his best works so penetrated by the spirit of the North, that through him it has, as it were, ascended upon all nations. In foreign countries he is not so much appreciated. The works by which he is best known are Correggio and Aladdin;

but assuredly his masterly poem of The Northern
Gods occupies a far higher rank : it is our Iliad.
It possesses power, freshness—nay, any expression
of mine is poor. It is possessed of grandeur ;
it is the poet Oehlenschläger in the blood of his
soul. Hakon Jarl, and Palnatoke will live in
the poetry of Oehlenschläger as long as mankind
endures. Denmark, Norway, and Sweden have
fully appreciated him, and have shown him that
they do so, and whenever it is asked who occupies
the first place in the kingdom of mind, the palm is
always awarded to him. He is the true-born
poet ; he appears always young, whilst he himself,
the oldest of all, surpasses all the productiveness
of his mind.

He listened with friendly disposition to my
first lyrical outpourings ; and he acknowledged
with earnestness and cordiality the poet who told
the fairy-tales. My Biographer in the Danish
Pantheon, brought me in contact with Oehlenschläger, when he said, "In our days it is becoming
more and more rare for any one, by implicitly
following those inborn impulses of his soul, which
make themselves irresistibly felt, to step forward
as an artist or a poet. He is more frequently

fashioned by fate and circumstances than apparently destined by nature herself for this office. With the greatest number of our poets an early acquaintance with passion, early inward experience, or outward circumstances, stand instead of the original vein of nature, and this cannot in any case be more incontestably proved in our own literature than by instancing Oehlenschläger and Andersen. And in this way it may be explained why the former has been so frequently the object for the attacks of the critics, and why the latter was first properly appreciated as a poet in foreign countries where civilisation of a longer date has already produced a disinclination for the compulsory rule of schools, and has occasioned a reaction towards that which is fresh and natural ; whilst we Danes, on the contrary, cherish a pious respect for the yoke of the schools and the worn-out wisdom of maxims."

Thorwaldsen, whom, as I have already said, I had become acquainted with in Rome in the years 1833 and 1834, was expected in Denmark in the autumn of 1838, and great festive preparations were made in consequence. A flag was to wave upon one of the towers of Copenhagen as soon as the vessel which brought him should come in sight. It was a national festival. Boats decorated with flowers and flags filled the Rhede ; painters, sculptors, all had their flags with emblems ; the students' bore a Minerva, the poets' a Pegasus. It was misty weather, and the ship was first seen when it was already close by the city, and all poured out to meet him. The poets, who, I believe, according to the arrangement of Heiberg, had been invited, stood by their boat ; Oehlenschläger and Heiberg alone had not arrived. And now guns were fired from the ship, which came to anchor, and it was to be feared that Thorwaldsen might land before we had gone out to meet him. The wind bore the voice of singing over to us : the festive reception had already began.

I wished to see him, and therefore cried out to the others, "Let us put off ! "

" Without Oehlenschläger and Heiberg ? " asked some one.

" But they have not arrived, and it will be all over. "

One of the poets declared that if these two men were not with us, I should not sail under that flag, and pointed up to Pegasus.

"We will throw it in the boat," said I, and took it down from the staff; the others now followed me, and came up just as Thorwaldsen reached land. We met with Oehlenschläger and Heiberg in another boat, and they came over to us as the enthusiasm began on shore.

The people drew Thorwaldsen's carriage through the streets to his house, where everybody who had the slightest acquaintance with him, or with the friends of a friend of his, thronged around him. In the evening the artists gave him a serenade, and the blaze of the torches illumined the garden under the large trees, there was an exultation and joy which really and truly was felt. Young and old hastened through the open doors, and the joyful old man clasped those whom he knew to his breast, gave them his kiss, and pressed their hands. There was a glory round Thorwaldsen which kept me timidly back: my heart beat for joy of seeing him who had met me when abroad with kindness and consolation, who had pressed me to his heart, and had said that we must always remain friends. But here in this jubilant crowd, where thousands noticed every movement of his, where I too by all these should be observed and criticised—yes, criticised as a vain man who now only wished to show that he too was acquainted with Thorwaldsen, and that this great man was kind and friendly towards him—here, in this dense crowd, I drew myself back, and avoided being recognised by him. Some days afterwards, and early in the morning, I went to call upon him, and found him as a friend who had wondered at not having seen me earlier.

In honour of Thorwaldsen, a musical-poetic academy was established, and the poets, who were invited to do so by Heiberg, wrote and read each one a poem in praise of him who had returned home. I wrote of Jason who fetched the golden fleece—that is to say, Jason-Thorwaldsen, who went forth to win golden art. A great dinner and a ball closed the festival, in which, for the first time in Denmark, popular life and a subject of great interest in the realms of art were made public.

From this evening I saw Thorwaldsen almost daily in company or in his studio : I often passed several weeks together with him at Nysö where he seemed to have firmly taken root, and where the greater number of his works, executed in Denmark, had their origin. He was of a healthful and simple disposition of mind, not without humour, and therefore, he was extremely attached to Holberg the poet : he did not at all enter into the troubles and the disruptions of the world.

One morning at Nysö—at the time when he was working at his own statue—I entered his work-room and bade him good morning ; he appeared as if he did not wish to notice me, and I stole softly away again. At breakfast he was very parsimonious in the use of words, and when somebody asked him to say something at all events, he replied in his dry way :—

" I have said more during this morning than in many whole days, but nobody heard me. There I stood, and fancied that Andersen was behind me, for he came, and said good morning—so I told him a long story about myself and Byron. I thought that he might give one word in reply, and turned myself round ; and there had I been standing a whole hour and chattering aloud to the bare walls."

We all of us besought him to let us hear the whole story once more ; but he did it now very short.

" Oh, that was in Rome," said he, " when I was about to make Byron's statue ; he placed himself just opposite to me and began immediately to assume quite another countenance to what was customary to him. Will not you sit still ? said I ; but you must not make these faces. It is my expression, said Byron. Indeed ? said I, and then I made him as I wished, and everybody said when it was finished, that I had hit the likeness.

When Byron, however, saw it, he said, "It does not resemble me at all : I look more unhappy."

" He was, above all things, so desirous of looking extremely unhappy," added Thorwaldsen, with a comic expression.

It afforded the great sculptor pleasure to listen to music after dinner with half-shut eyes, and it was his greatest delight when in the evening the game of lotto began, which the whole neighbour-hood of Nysö was obliged to learn ; they only played for glass pieces, and on this account I am able to relate a peculiar characteristic of this otherwise great man—that he played with the greatest interest on purpose to win.

He would espouse with warmth and vehemence the part of those from whom he believed that he had received an injustice ; he opposed himself to unfairness and raillery, even against the lady of the house, who for the rest had the most childlike sentiments towards him, and who had no other thought than how to make every thing most agreeable to him.

In his company I wrote several of my tales for children—for example, " Ole Luköie " ("Ole Shut Eye,")to which he listened with pleasure and interest. Often in the twilight, when the family circle sate in the open garden parlour, Thorwaldsen would come softly behind me, and, clapping me on the shoulder, would ask, " Shall we little ones hear any tales to-night ? "

In his own peculiarly natural manner he bestowed the most bountiful praise on my fictions, for their truth ; it delighted him to hear the same stories over and over again. Often, during his most glorious works, would he stand with laughing countenance, and listen to the stories of the Top and the Ball, and the Ugly Duckling. I possess a certain talent of improvising in my native tongue little poems and songs. This talent amused Thorwaldsen very much ; and as he had modelled, at Nysö, Holberg's portrait in clay, I was commissioned to make a poem for his work,

and he received, therefore, the following im-
promptu :—

> "No more shall Holberg live" by Death was said,
>   "I crush the clay, his soul's bonds heretofore."
> "And from the formless clay, the cold, the dead,"
>   Cried Thorwaldsen, "shall Holberg live once more

One morning when he had just modelled in clay
his great bas-relief of the Procession to Golgotha,
I entered his study.

"Tell me," said he, "does it seem to you that
I have dressed Pilate properly ? "

"You must not say any thing to him," said the
Baroness, who was always with him : "it is right ;
it is excellent ; go away with you ! "

Thorwaldsen repeated his question.

"Well then," said I, "as you ask me, I must
confess that it really does appear to me as if Pilate
were dressed rather as an Egyptian than as a
Roman."

"It seems to me so too," said Thorwaldsen,
seizing the clay with his hand, and destroying
the figure.

"Now you are guilty of his having annihilated
an immortal work," exclained the Baroness to
me with warmth.

" Then we can make a new immortal work," said he, in a cheerful humour, and modelled Pilate as he now remains in the bas-relief in Our Lady's Church in Copenhagen.

His last birth-day was celebrated there in the country. I had written a merry little song, and it was hardly dry on the paper, when we sang it, in the early morning, just before his door, accompanied by the music of jingling fire-irons, gongs, and bottles rubbed against a basket. Thorwaldsen himself, in his morning gown and slippers, opened his door, and danced round his chamber; swung round his Raphael's cap, and joined in the chorus. There was life and mirth in the strong old man.

On the last day of his life I sate by him at dinner; he was unusually good humoured; repeated several witticisms which he had just read in the Corsair, a well-known Copenhagen newspaper, and spoke of the journey which he should undertake to Italy in the summer. After this we parted; he went to the theatre, and I home.

On the following morning the waiter at the hotel where I lived said, " that it was a very remarkable thing about Thorwaldsen—that he had died yesterday."

" Thorwaldsen ! " exclaimed I ; " he is not dead, I dined with him yesterday."

" People say that he died last evening at the theatre," returned the waiter.

I fancied that he might be taken ill ; but still I felt a strange anxiety, and hastened immediately over to his house. There lay his corpse stretched out on the bed ; the chamber was filled with strangers ; the floor wet with melted snow ; the air stifling ; no one said a word : the Baroness Stampe sate on the bed and wept bitterly. I stood trembling and deeply agitated.

A farewell hymn, which I wrote, and to which Hartmann composed the music, was sung by Danish students over his coffin.

CHAPTER VII

In the summer of 1842, I wrote a little piece for the summer theatre, called " The Bird in the Pear-tree," in which several scenes were acted up in the pear-tree. I had called it a dramatic trifle, in order that no one might expect either a great work or one of a very elaborate character. It was a little sketch, which, after being performed a few times, was received with so much applause, that the directors of the theatre accepted it : nay, even Mrs. Heiberg, the favourite of the public, desired to take a part in it. People had amused themselves ; had thought the selection of the music excellent. I knew that the piece had stood its rehearsal—and then suddenly it was hissed. Some young men, who gave the word to hiss, had said to some others, who inquired from them their reasons for doing so, that the trifle had too much luck, and then Andersen would be getting too mettlesome.

I was not, on this evening, at the theatre myself, and had not the least idea of what was going on.

On the following day I went to the house of one of my friends. I had head-ache, and was looking very grave. The lady of the house met me with a sympathising manner, took my hand, and said, " Is it really worth while to take it so much to heart ? There were only two hissed, the whole house beside took your part."

" Hissed ! My part ! Have I been hissed ? " exclaimed I.

It was quite comic ; one person assured me that this hissing had been a triumph for me ; everybody had joined in acclamation, and " there was only one who hissed."

After this another person came and I asked him of the number of those who hissed. " Two," said he. The next person said three," and said positively there were no more. One of my most veracious friends now made his appearance, and I asked him, upon his conscience, how many he had heard ; he laid his hand upon his heart, and said that, at the very highest, they were five.

" No," said I, " now I will ask nobody more ; the numbers grows just as with Falstaff ; here stands one who asserts that there was only one person who hissed."

Shocked, and yet inclined to set it all right again, he replied, " Yes, that is possible, but then it was a strong, powerful hiss."

By my last works, and through a rational economy, I had now saved a small sum of money, which I had destined to the purposes of a new journey to Paris, where I arrived in the winter of 1843, by way of Dusseldorf, through Belgium.

Marmier had already, in the *Révue de Paris*, written an article on me, *La Vie d'un Poète*. He had also translated several of my poems into French, and had actually honoured me with a poem which is printed in the above-named *Révue*. My name had thus reached, like a sound, the ears of some persons in the literary world, and I here met with a surprisingly friendly reception.

At Victor Hugo's invitation, I saw his abused *Burggraves*. Mr. and Mrs. Ancelot opened their house to me, and there I met Martinez della Rosa and other remarkable men of these times. Lamartine seemed to me, in his domestic, and in his whole personal appearance, as the prince of them all. On my apologising because I spoke such bad French, he replied, that he was to blame, because he did not understand the northern languages, in which, as he had discovered in late years, their existed a fresh and vigorous literature, and where the poetical ground was so peculiar that you had only to stoop down to find an old golden horn. He asked about the Trollhätta canal, and avowed a wish to visit Denmark and Stockholm. He recollected also our now reigning king, to whom, when as prince he was in Castellamare, he had paid his respects ; besides this, he exhibited, for a Frenchman, an extraordinary acquaintance with names and places in Denmark. On my departure he wrote a little poem for me, which I preserve amongst my dearest relics.

I generally found the jovial Alexander Dumas in bed, even long after mid-day: here he lay, with paper, pen, and ink, and wrote his newest drama. I found him thus one day ; he nodded kindly to me, and said, " Sit down a minute ; I have just now a visit from my muse ; she will be going directly. He wrote on ; spoke aloud ; shouted a *viva*! sprang out of bed, and said, " The third act is finished ! "

One evening he conducted me round into the various theatres, that I might see the life behind the scenes. We wandered about, arm in arm, along the gay Boulevard.

I also have to thank him for my acquaintance with Rachel. I had not seen her act, when Alexander Dumas asked me whether I had the desire to make her acquaintance. One evening, when she was to come out as Phedra he led me to the stage of the Théâtre Français. The representation had begun, and behind the scenes, where a folding screen had formed a sort of room, in which stood a table with refreshments, and a few ottomans, sate the young girl who, as an author has said, understands how to chisel living statues out of Racine's and Corneille's blocks of marble. She was thin and slenderly formed, and looked very young. She looked to me there, and more particularly so afterwards in her own house, as an image of mourning ; as a young girl who has just wept out her sorrow, and will now let her thoughts repose in quiet. She accosted us kindly in a deep powerful voice. In the course of conversation with Dumas, she forgot me. I stood there quite superfluous. Dumas observed it, said something handsome of me, and on that I ventured to take part in the discourse, although I had a depressing feeling that I stood before those who perhaps spoke the most beautiful French in all

France. I said that I truly had seen much that was glorious and interesting, but that I never yet had seen a Rachel, and that on her account especially had I devoted the profits of my last work to a journey to Paris ; and as, in conclusion, I added an apology on account of my French, she smiled and said, " When you say any thing so polite as that which you have just said to me, to a Frenchwoman, she will always think that you speak well."

When I told her that her fame had resounded to the North, she declared that it was her intention to go to Petersburg and Copenhagen ; " and when I come to your city," she said, " you must be my defender, as you are the only one there whom I know ; and in order that we may become acquainted, and as you, as you say, are come to Paris especially on my account, we must see one another frequently. You will be welcome to me. I see my friends at my house every Thursday. But duty calls," said she, and offering us her hand she nodded kindly, and then stood a few paces from us on the stage, taller, quite different, and with the expression of the tragic muse herself. Joyous acclamations ascended to where we sate.

As a Northlander I cannot accustom myself to the French mode of acting tragedy. Rachel plays in this same style, but in her it appears to be nature itself ; it is as if all the others strove to imitate her. She is herself the French tragic muse, the others are only poor human beings. When Rachel plays, people fancy that all tragedy must be acted in this manner. It is in her truth and nature, but under another revelation to that which we are acquainted in the north.

At her house everything is rich and magnificent, perhaps too *recherché*. The innermost room was blue-green, with shaded lamps and statuettes of French authors. In her salon, properly speaking, the colour which prevailed principally in the carpets, curtains, and bookcases was crimson. She herself was dressed in black, probably as she is represented in the well-known English steel engraving of her. Her guests consisted of gentlemen, for the greater part artists and men of learning. I also heard a few titles amongst them. Richly apparelled servants announced the names of the arrivals : tea was drunk and refreshments handed round, more in the German than the French style.

Victor Hugo had told me that he found she
understood the German language. I asked her,
and she replied in German, " ich kann es lesen ;
ich bin ja in Lothringen geboren ; ich habe deutsche
Bücher, sehn Sie hier ! " and she showed me
Grillparzer's " Sappho," and she immediately
continued the conversation in French. She expressed her pleasure in acting the part of Sappho,
and then spoke of Schiller's " Maria Stuart," which
character she has personated in a French version
of that play. I saw her in this part, and she gave
the last act especially with such a composure and
tragic feeling, that she might have been one of the
best of German actresses ; but it was precisely in
this very act that the French liked her least.

" My countrymen," said she, " are not accustomed to this manner, and in this manner alone
can the part be given. No one should be raving
when the heart is almost broken with sorrow, and
when he is about to take an everlasting farewell
of his friends."

Her drawing-room was for the most part,
decorated with books which were splendidly bound
and arranged in handsome book-cases behind
glass. A painting hung on the wall, which

represented the interior of the theatre in London, where she stood forward on the stage, and flowers and garlands were thrown to her across the orchestra. Below this picture hung a pretty little book-shelf, holding what I call "the high nobility among the poets,"—Goethe, Schiller, Calderon, Shakspeare, &c.

She asked me many questions respecting Germany and Denmark, art, and the theatre; and she encouraged me with a kind smile around her grave mouth, when I stumbled in French and stopped for a moment to collect myself, that I might not stick quite fast.

"Only speak," said she. "It is true that you do not speak French well. I have heard many foreigners speak my native language better; but their conversation has not been nearly as interesting as yours. I understand the sense of your words perfectly, and that is the principal thing which interests me in you."

The last time we parted she wrote the following words in my album: "L'art c'est le vrai! J'espére que cet aphorisme ne semblera pas paradoxal à un écrivain si distingué comme M. Andersen."

I perceived amiability of character in Alfred de Vigny. He has married an English lady, and that which is best in both nations seemed to unite in his house. The last evening which I spent in Paris, he himself, who is possessed of intellectual status and worldly wealth, came almost at midnight to my lodging in the Rue Richelieu, ascended the many steps, and brought me his works under his arm. So much cordiality beamed in his eyes and he seemed to be so full of kindness towards me, that I felt affected by our separation.

I also became acquainted with the sculptor David. There was something in his demeanour and in his straightforward manner that reminded me of Thorwaldsen and Bissen, especially of the latter. We did not meet till towards the conclusion of my residence in Paris. He lamented it, and said that he would execute a bust for me if I would remain there longer.

When I said, " But you know nothing of me as a poet, and cannot tell whether I deserve it or not," he looked earnestly in my face, clapped me on the shoulder, and said, " I have, however, read you yourself before your books. You are a poet."

At the Countess——'s, where I met with Balzac,

I saw an old lady, the expression of whose countenance attracted my attention. There was something so animated, so cordial in it, and every body gathered about her. The Countess introduced me to her, and I heard that she was Madame Reybaud, the authoress of Les Epaves, the little story which I had made use of for my little drama of The Mulatto. I told her all about it, and of the representation of the piece, which interested her so much, that she became from this evening my especial protectress. We went out one evening together and exchanged ideas. She corrected my French and allowed me to repeat what did not appear correct to her. She is a lady of rich mental endowments, with a clear insight into the world, and she showed maternal kindness towards me.

I also again met with Heine. He had married since I was last here. I found him in indifferent health ; but full of energy, and so friendly and so natural in his behaviour towards me, that I felt no timidity in exhibiting myself to him as I was. One day he had been relating to his wife my story of the Constant Tin Soldier, and, whilst he said that I was the author of this story, he introduced me to her. She was a lively, pretty young lady. A troop of children, who, as Heine says, belonged to a neighbour, played about in their room. We two played with them whilst Heine copied out one of his last poems for me.

I perceived in him no pain-giving, sarcastic smile; I only heard the pulsation of a German heart, which is always perceptible in the songs, and which *must* live.

Through the means of the many people I was acquainted with here, among whom I might enumerate many others, as, for instance, Kalkbrenner, Gathy, &c., my residence in Paris was made very cheerful and rich in pleasure. I did not feel myself like a stranger there : I met with a friendly reception among the greatest and best. It was like a payment by anticipation of the talent which was in me, and through which they expected that I would some time prove them not to have been mistaken.

Whilst I was in Paris, I received from Germany, where already several of my works were translated and read, a delightful and encouraging proof of friendship. A German family, one of the most highly cultivated and amiable with whom I am acquainted, had read my writings with interest, especially the little biographical sketch prefixed to Only a Fiddler, and felt the heartiest goodwill towards me, with whom they were then not personally acquainted. They wrote to me, expressed their thanks for my works and the pleasure they had derived from them, and offered me a kind welcome to their house if I would visit it on my return home. There was a something extremely cordial and natural in this letter, which was the first that I received of this kind in Paris, and it also formed a remarkable contrast to that which was sent to me from my native land in the year 1833, when I was here for the first time.

In this way I found myself, through my writings, adopted, as it were, into a family to which since then I gladly betake myself, and where I know that it is not as the poet, but as the man, that I am beloved. In how many instances have I not experienced the same kindness in foreign countries! I will mention one for the sake of its peculiarity.

There lived in Saxony a wealthy and benevolent family; the lady of the house read my romance of Only a Fiddler, and the impression of this book was such that she vowed that, if ever, in the course of her life, she should meet with a poor child which was possessed of great musical talents, she would not allow it to perish as the poor Fiddler had done. A musician who had heard her say this, brought to her soon after, not one, but two poor boys, assuring her of their talent and reminding her of her promise. She kept her word; both boys were received into her house, were educated by her, and are now in the Conservatorium; the youngest of them played before me, and I saw that his countenance was happy and joyful. The same thing perhaps might have happened; the same excellent lady might have befriended these children without my book having been written: but notwithstanding this, my book is now connected with this as a link in the chain.

On my return home from Paris, I went along the Rhine; I knew that the poet Freiligrath, to whom the King of Prussia had given a pension, was residing in one of the Rhine towns. The picturesque character of his poems had delighted me extremely, and I wished to talk with him. I stopped at several towns on the Rhine and inquired after him. In St. Goar, I was shown the house in which he lived. I found him sitting at his writing table, and he appeared annoyed at being disturbed by a stranger. I did not mention my name ; but merely said that I could not pass St. Goar without paying my respects to the poet Freiligrath.

" That is very kind of you," said he, in a very cold tone ; and then asked who I was.

" We have both of us one and the same friend, Chamisso ! " replied I, and at these words he leapt up exultantly.

" You are then Andersen ! " he exclaimed ; threw his arms around my neck, and his honest eyes beamed with joy.

" Now you will stop several days here," said he. I told him that I could stay a couple of hours, because I was travelling with some of my country-men who were waiting for me.

" You have a great many friends in little St. Goar," said he ; " it is but a short time since I read aloud your novel of O.T. to a large circle ; one of these friends I must, at all events, fetch here, and you must also see my wife. Yes, indeed, you do not know that you had something to do in our being married."

He then related to me how my novel, Only a

Fiddler, had caused them to exchange letters, and then led to their acquaintance, which acquaintance had ended in their being a married couple. He called her, mentioned to her my name, and I was regarded as an old friend. Such moments as these are a blessing ; a mercy of God, a happiness—and how many such, how various, have I not enjoyed !

I relate all these, to me, joyful occurrences ; they are facts in my life : I relate them, as I formerly have related that which was miserable, humiliating, and depressing ; and if I have done so, in the spirit which operated in my soul, it will not be called pride or vanity ;—neither of them would assuredly be the proper name for it. But people may perhaps ask at home, Has Andersen then never been attacked in foreign countries ? I must reply,—no !

No regular attack has been made upon me, at least they have never at home called my attention to any such, and therefore there certainly cannot have been any thing of the kind ;—with the exception of one which made its appearance in Germany, but which originated in Denmark, at the very moment I was in Paris.

A certain Mr. Boas made a journey at that time through Scandinavia, and wrote a book on the subject.   In this he gave a sort of survey of Danish literature, which he also published in the journal called Die Grenzboten ; in this I was very severely handled as a man and as a poet.   Several other Danish poets also, as for instance, Christian Winter, have an equally great right to complain.   Mr. Boas had drawn his information out of the miserable gossip of everyday life : his work excited attention in Copenhagen and nobody there would allow themselves to be considered as his informants ; nay even Holst the poet, who, as may be seen from the work, travelled with him through Sweden, and had received him at his house in Copenhagen, on this occasion published, in one of the most widely circulated of our papers, a declaration that he was in no way connected with Mr. Boas.

Mr. Boas had in Copenhagen attached himself to a particular clique consisting of a few young men ; he had heard them full of lively spirits, talking during the day, of the Danish poets and their writings ; he had then gone home, written down what he had heard and afterwards published it in his work.   This was, to use the mildest term, inconsiderate. That my Improvisatore and Only a Fiddler did not please him, is a matter of taste, and to that I must submit myself. But when he, before the whole of Germany, where probably people will presume that what he has written is true, if he declare it to be, as is the case, the universal judgment against me in my native land; when he, I say, declared me before the whole of Germany, to be the most haughty of men, he inflicts upon me a deeper wound than he perhaps imagined. He conveyed the voice of a party, formerly hostile to me, into foreign countries. Nor is he true even in that which he represents he gives circumstances as facts, which never took place.

In Denmark what he has written could not injure me, and many have declared themselves afraid of coming into contact with any one, who printed everything which he heard. His book was read in Germany, the public of which is now also mine; and I believe, therefore, that I may here say how faulty is his view of Danish literature and Danish poets; in what manner his book was received in my native land and that people there know in what way it was put together. But after

I have expressed myself thus on this subject I will gladly offer Mr. Boas my hand ; and if, in his next visit to Denmark, no other poet will receive him, I will do my utmost for him ; I know that he will not be able to judge me more severely when we know each other, than when we knew each other not. His judgment would also have been quite of another character had he come to Denmark but one year later ; things changed very much in a year's time. Then the tide had turned in my favour ; I then had published my new children's stories, of which from that moment to the present there prevailed, through the whole of my native land, but one unchanging honourable opinion. When the edition of my collection of stories came out at Christmas 1843, the reaction began ; acknowledgment of my merits were made, and favour shown me in Denmark, and from that time I have no cause for complaint. I have obtained and I obtain in my own land that which I deserve, nay perhaps, much more.

I will now turn to those little stories which in Denmark have been placed by everyone, without any hesitation, higher than anything else I had hitherto written.

In the year 1835, some months after I published the Improvisatore, I brought out my first volume of Stories for Children,* which at that time was not so very much thought of. One monthly critical journal even complained that a young author who had just published a work like the Improvisatore, should immediately come out with anything so childish as the tales. I reaped a harvest of blame, precisely where people ought to have acknowledged the advantage of my mind producing something in a new direction. Several of my friends, whose judgment was of value to me, counselled me entirely to abstain from writing tales, as these were a something for which I had no talent. Others were of opinion that I had better, first of all, study the French fairy tale. I would willingly have discontinued writing them, but they forced themselves from me.

In the volume which I first published, I had, like Musäus, but in my own manner, related old stories, which I had heard as a child. The volume

* I find it very difficult to give a correct translation of the original word. The Danish is *Eventyr*, equivalent to the German *Abentheur*, or adventure; but adventures give in English a very different idea to this class of stories. The German word *Marchen*, gives the meaning completely and this we may English by *fairy tale* or *legend*, but then neither of these works are fully correct with regard to Andersen's stories. In my translation of his "Eventyr fortalte for Born," I gave as an equivalent title "Wonderful Stories for Children," and perhaps this was as near as I could come.—M. H.

concluded with one which was original, and which seemed to have given the greatest pleasure although it bore a tolerably near affinity to a story of Hoffman's. In my increasing disposition for children's stories, I therefore followed my own impulse, and invented them myself. In the following year a new volume came out, and soon after that a third, in which the longest story, The Little Mermaid, was my own invention. This story, in an especial manner, created an interest which was only increased by the following volumes. One of these came out every Christmas, and before long no Christmas tree could exist without my stories.

Some of our first comic actors made the attempt of relating my little stories from the stage; it was a complete change from the declamatory poetry which had been heard to satiety. The Constant Tin Soldier, therefore, the Swineherd, and the Top and Ball, were told from the Royal stage, and from those of private theatres, and were well received. In order that the reader might be placed in the proper point of view, with regard to the manner in which I told the stories, I had called my first volume Stories told for Children. I had written my narrative down upon paper, exactly in the language, and with the expressions in which I had myself related them, by word of mouth, to the little ones, and I had arrived at the conviction that people of different ages were equally amused with them. The children made themselves merry for the most part over what might be called the actors, older people, on the contrary, were interested in the deeper meaning. The stories furnished reading for children and grown people, and that assuredly is a difficult task for those who will write children's stories. They met with open doors and open hearts in Denmark; every body read them. I now removed the words "told for children," from my title, and published three volumes of "New Stories," all of which were of my own invention, and which were received in my own country with the greatest favour. I could not wish it greater; I felt a real anxiety in consequence, a fear of not being able to justify afterwards such an honourable award of praise.

A refreshing sunshine streamed into my heart; I felt courage and joy, and was filled with a living desire of still more and more developing my powers in this direction,—of studying more thoroughly this class of writing, and of observing still more attentively the rich wells of nature out of which I must create it. If attention be paid to the order in which my stories are written, it certainly will be seen that there is in them a gradual progression, clearer working out of the idea, a greater discretion in the use of agency, and, if I may so speak, a more healthy tone and a more natural freshness may be perceived.

At this period of my life, I made an acquaintance which was of great moral and intellectual importance to me. I have already spoken of several persons and public characters who have had influence on me as the poet ; but none of these have had more, nor in a nobler sense of the word, than the lady to whom I here turn myself ; she, through whom I, at the same time, was enabled to forget my own individual self, to feel that which is holy in art, and to become acquainted with the command which God has given to genius.

I now turn back to the year 1840. One day in the hotel in which I lived in Copenhagen, I saw the name of Jenny Lind among those of the strangers from Sweden. I was aware at that time that she was the first singer in Stockholm. I had been that same year, in this neighbour country, and had there met with honour and kindness : I thought, therefore, that it would not be unbecoming to me to pay a visit to the young artist. She was, at this time, entirely unknown out of Sweden, so that I was convinced that, even in Copenhagen, her name was known only by few. She received me very courteously, but yet distantly, almost coldly. She was, as she said, on a journey with her father to South Sweden, and was come over to Copenhagen for a few days in order that she might see this city. We again parted distantly, and I had the impression of a very ordinary character which soon passed away from my mind.

In the autumn of 1843, Jenny Lind came again to Copenhagen. One of my friends, our clever ballet-master, Bournonville, who has married a Swedish lady, a friend of Jenny Lind, informed me of her arrival here and told me that she remembered me very kindly, and that now she had read my writings. He entreated me to go with him to her, and to employ all my persuasive art to induce her to take a few parts at the Theatre Royal ; I should, he said, be then quite enchanted with what I should hear.

I was not now received as a stranger; she cordially extended to me her hand, and spoke of my writings and of Miss Fredrika Bremer, who also was her affectionate friend. The conversation was soon turned to her appearance in Copenhagen, and of this Jenny Lind declared that she stood in fear.

" I have never made my appearance," said she, "Out of Sweden ; every body in my native land is so affectionate and kind to me, and if I made my appearance in Copenhagen and should be hissed !—I dare not venture on it ! "

I said, that I, it was true, could not pass judgment on her singing, because I had never heard it, neither did I know how she acted, but nevertheless I was convinced that such was the disposition at this moment in Copenhagen, that only a moderate voice and some knowledge of acting would be successful ; I believed that she might safely venture.

Bournonville's persuasion obtained for the Copenhageners the greatest enjoyment which they ever had.

Jenny Lind made her first appearance among them as Alice in Robert le Diable—it was like a new revelation in the realms of art, the youthfully

JENNY LIND
From a Painting by Erwin Magnus, 1846

fresh voice forced itself into every heart ; here reigned truth and nature ; every thing was full of meaning and intelligence. At one concert Jenny Lind sang her Swedish songs ; there was something so peculiar in this, so bewitching ; people thought nothing about the concert room ; the popular melodies uttered by a being so purely feminine, and bearing the universal stamp of genius, exercised their omnipotent sway—the whole of Copenhagen was in raptures. Jenny Lind was the first singer to whom the Danish students gave a serenade : torches blazed round the hospitable villa where the serenade was given : she expressed her thanks by again singing some Swedish songs, and then I saw her hasten into the darkest corner and weep for emotion.

"Yes, yes," said she, "I will exert myself ; I will endeavour, I will be better qualified than I am when I again come to Copenhagen."

On the stage, she was the great artiste, who rose above all those around her ; at home, in her own chamber, a sensitive young girl with all the humility and piety of a child.

Her appearance in Copenhagen made an epoch in the history of our opera ; it showed me art in its sanctity—I had beheld one of its vestals. She journeyed back to Stockholm, and from there Fredrika Bremer wrote to me :—" With regard to Jenny Lind as a singer, we were both of us perfectly agreed ; she stands as high as any artist of our time can stand ; but as yet you do not know her in her full greatness. Speak to her about her art, and you will wonder at the expansion of her mind, and you will see her countenance beaming with inspiration. Converse then with her of God, and of the holiness of religion, and you will see tears in those innocent eyes ; she is great as an artist, but she is still greater in her pure human existence ! "

In the following year I was in Berlin ; the conversation with Meyerbeer turned upon Jenny Lind ; he had heard her sing the Swedish songs and was transported by them.

" But how does she act ? " asked he.

I spoke in raptures of her acting, and gave him at the same time some idea of her representation of Alice. He said to me that perhaps it might be possible for him to determine her to come to Berlin.

It is sufficiently well known that she made her

appearance there, threw every one into astonishment and delight, and won for herself in Germany,
a European name. Last autumn she came again
to Copenhagen, and the enthusiasm was incredible ;
the glory of renown makes genius perceptible
to every one. People bivouacked regularly before
the theatre, to obtain a ticket. Jenny Lind
appeared still greater than ever in her art, because
they had an opportunity of seeing her in many
and such extremely different parts. Her Norma
is plastic ; every attitude might serve as the most
beautiful model to a sculptor, and yet people
felt that these were the inspiration of the moment,
and had not been studied before the glass. Norma
is no raving Italian ; she is the suffering, sorrowing
woman—the woman possessed of a heart to
sacrifice herself for an unfortunate rival—the
woman to whom, in the violence of the moment,
the thought may suggest itself of murdering the
children of a faithless lover, but who is immediately
disarmed when she gazes into the eyes of the
innocent ones.

" Norma, thou holy priestess," sings the chorus,
and Jenny Lind has comprehended and shows to
us this holy priestess in the aria, *Casta diva*. In

Copenhagen she sang all her parts in Swedish, and the other singers sang theirs in Danish, and the two kindred languages mingled very beautifully together; there was no jarring; even in the Daughter of the Regiment, where there is a deal of dialogue, the Swedish had something agreeable —and what acting! nay, the word itself is a contradiction—it was nature; anything as true never before appeared on the stage. She shows us perfectly the true child of nature grown up in the camp, but an inborn nobility pervades every movement. The Daughter of the Regiment and the Somnambule are certainly Jenny Lind's most unsurpassable parts; no second can take their places in these beside her. People laugh,—they cry; it does them as much good as going to church; they become better for it. People feel that God is in art; and where God stands before us face to face there is a holy church.

"There will not in a whole century," said Mendelssohn, speaking to me of Jenny Lind, " be born another being so gifted as she;" and his words expressed my full conviction; one feels as she makes her appearance on the stage, that she is a pure vessel, from which a holy draught will be presented to us.

There is not any thing which can lessen the impression which Jenny Lind's greatness on the stage makes, except her own personal character at home. An intelligent and child-like disposition exercises here its astonishing power ; she is happy ; belonging, as it were, no longer to the world, a peaceful, quiet home, is the object of her thoughts —and yet she loves art with her whole soul, and feels her vocation in it. A noble, pious disposition like hers cannot be spoiled by homage. On one occasion only did I hear her express her joy in her talent and her self-consciousness. It was during her last residence in Copenhagen. Almost every evening she appeared either in the opera or at concerts ; every hour was in requisition. She heard of a society, the object of which was, to assist unfortunate children, and to take them out of the hands of their parents by whom they were misused, and compelled either to beg or steal, and to place them in other and better circum-stances. Benevolent people subscribed annually a small sum each for their support, nevertheless the means for this excellent purpose were small.

" But have I not still a disengaged evening ? " said she ; " let me give a night's performance for the benefit of these poor children ; but we will have double prices ! "

Such a performance was given, and returned large proceeds ; when she was informed of this, and, that by this means, a number of poor children would be benefited for several years, her countenance beamed, and the tears filled her eyes.

" It is however beautiful," said she, " that I can sing so ! "

I value her with the whole feeling of a brother, and I regard myself as happy that I know and understand such a spirit. God give to her that peace, that quiet happiness which she wishes for herself ! "

Through Jenny Lind I first became sensible of the holiness there is in art ; through her I learned that one must forget oneself in the service of the Supreme. No books, no men have had a better or a more ennobling influence on me as the poet, than Jenny Lind, and I therefore have spoken of her so long and so warmly here.

I have made the happy discovery by experience, that inasmuch as art and life are more clearly understood by me, so much more sunshine from without has streamed into my soul. What blessings have not compensated me for the former dark days! Repose and certainty have forced themselves into my art. Such repose can easily unite itself with the changing life of travel; I feel myself everywhere at home, attach myself to people, and they give me in return confidence and cordiality.

In the summer of 1844 I once more visited North Germany. An intellectual and amiable family in Oldenburg had invited me in the most friendly manner to spend some time at their house. Count von Rantzau-Breitenburg repeated also in his letters how welcome I should be to him. I set out on the journey, and this journey was, if not one of my longest, still one of my most interesting.

I saw the rich marsh-land in its summer luxuriance, and made with Rantzau several interesting little excursions. Breitenburg lies in the middle of woods on the river Stör; the steam-voyage to Hamburg gives animation to the little river; the situation is picturesque, and life in the castle itself is comfortable and pleasant. I could devote myself perfectly to reading and poetry, because

I was just as free as the bird in the air, and I was as much cared for as if I had been a beloved relation of the family. Alas, it was the last time that I came hither ; Count Rantzau had, even then, a presentiment of his approaching death. One day we met in the garden ; he seized my hand, pressed it warmly, expressed his pleasure in my talents being acknowledged abroad, and his friendship for me, adding, in conclusion, " Yes, my dear young friend, God only knows, but I have the firm belief that this year is the last time when we two shall meet here ; my days will soon have run out their full course.'' He looked at me with so grave an expression, that it touched my heart deeply, but I knew not what to say. We were near to the chapel ; he opened a little gate between some thick hedges, and we stood in a little garden, in which was a turfed grave and a seat beside it.

"Here you will find me, when you come the next time to Breitenburg," said he, and his sorrowful words were true. He died the following winter in Wiesbaden. I lost in him a friend, a protector, a noble excellent heart.

When I, on the first occasion, went to Germany, I visited the Hartz and the Saxon Switzerland.

Goethe was still living. It was my most heartfelt wish to see him. It was not far from the Hartz to Weimar, but I had no letters of introduction to him, and, at that time, not one line of my writings was translated. Many persons had described Goethe to me as a very proud man, and the question arose whether he indeed would receive me. I doubted it, and determined not to go to Weimar until I should have written some work which would convey my name to Germany. I succeeded in this, but alas, Goethe was already dead.

I had made the acquaintance of his daughter-in-law Mrs. von Goethe, born Pogwisch, at the house of Mendelssohn Bartholdy, in Leipzig, on my return from Constantinople ; this *spirituelle* lady received me with much kindness. She told me that her son Walter had been my friend for a long time ; that as a boy he had made a whole play out of my Improvisatore ; that this piece had been performed in Goethe's house ; and lastly, that Walter had once wished to go to Copenhagen to make my acquaintance. I thus had now friends in Weimar.

An extraordinary desire impelled me to see this city where Goethe, Schiller, Wieland, and Herder had lived, and from which so much light had streamed forth over the world. I approached that land which had been rendered sacred by Luther, by the strife of the Minnesingers on the Wartburg, and by the memory of many noble and great events.

On the 24th of June, the birthday of the Grand Duke, I arrived a stranger in the friendly town. Every thing indicated the festivity which was then going forward, and the young prince was received with great rejoicing in the theatre, where a new opera was being given. I did not think how firmly, the most glorious and the best of all those whom I here saw around me, would grow into my heart ; how many of my future friends sate around me here—how dear this city would become to me— in Germany my second home. I was invited by Goethe's worthy friend, the excellent Chancellor Müller, and I met with the most cordial reception from him. By accident I here met, on my first call, with the Kammerherr Beaulieu de Marconnay, whom I had known in Oldenburg ; he was now placed in Weimar. He invited me to remove to his house. In the course of a few minutes I was his stationary guest, and I felt " it is good to be here."

There are people whom it only requires a few days to know and to love ; I won in Beaulieu, in these few days, a friend, as I believe, for my whole life. He introduced me into the family circle, the amiable chancellor received me equally cordially ; and I who had, on my arrival, fancied myself quite forlorn, because Mrs. von Goethe and her son Walter were in Vienna, was now known in Weimar, and well received in all its circles.

The reigning Grand Duke and Duchess gave me so gracious and kind a reception as made a deep impression upon me. After I had been presented, I was invited to dine, and soon after received an invitation to visit the hereditary Grand Duke and his lady, at the hunting seat of Ettersburg, which stands high, and close to an extensive forest. The old fashioned furniture within the house, and the distant views from the park in to the Hartz mountains, produced immediately a peculiar impression. All the young peasants had assembled at the castle to celebrate the birthday of their beloved young Duke ; climbing-poles, from which fluttered handkerchiefs and ribbons, were erected ; fiddles sounded, and people danced merrily under the branches of the large and flowering limetrees. Sabbath splendour, contentment and happiness were diffused over the whole.

The young and but new married princely pair seemed to be united by true heartfelt sentiment. The heart must be able to forget the star on the breast under which it beats, if its possessor wish to remain long and free and happy in a court; and such a heart, certainly one of the noblest and best which beats, is possessed by Karl Alexander of Saxe-Weimar. I had the happiness of a sufficient length of time to establish this belief. During this, my first residence here, I came several times to the happy Ettersburg. The young Duke showed me the garden and the tree on the trunk of which Goethe, Schiller, and Wieland had cut their names; nay even Jupiter himself had wished to add his to theirs, for his thunder-bolt had splintered it in one of the branches.

The intellectual Mrs. von Gross (Amalia Winter), Chancellor von Müller, who was able livingly to unroll the times of Goethe and to explain his Faust, and the soundly honest and child-like minded Eckermann belonged to the circle at Ettersburg. The evenings passed like a spiritual dream;

alternately some one read aloud ; even I ventured, for the first time in a foreign language to me, to read one of my own tales—the Constant Tin Soldier.

Chancellor von Müller accompanied me to the princely burial-place, where Karl August sleeps with his glorious wife, not between Schiller and Goethe, as I believed when I wrote—" the prince has made for himself a rainbow glory, whilst he stands between the sun and the rushing waterfall.'' Close beside the princely pair, who understood and valued that which was great, repose these their immortal friends, Withered laurel garlands lay upon the simple brown coffins, of which the whole magnificence consists in the immortal names of Goethe and Schiller. In life the prince and the poet walked side by side, in death they slumber under the same vault. Such a place as this is never effaced from the mind ; in such a spot those quiet prayers are offered, which God alone hears.

I remained above eight days in Weimar ; it seemed to me as if I had formerly lived in this city ; as if it were a beloved home which I must now leave. As I drove out of the city, over the bridge and past the mill, and for the last time looked back to the city and the castle, a deep melancholy

took hold on my soul, and it was to me as if a
beautiful portion of my life here had its close ;
I thought that the journey, after I had left Weimar,
could afford me no more pleasure. How often
since that time has the carrier pigeon, and still
more frequently, the mind, flown over to this place !
Sunshine has streamed forth from Weimar upon
my poet-life.

From Weimar I went to Leipzig where a truly
poetical evening awaited me with Robert
Schumann. This great composer had a year
before surprised me by the honour of dedicating
to me the music which he had composed to four
of my songs ; the lady of Dr. Frege whose singing,
so full of soul, has pleased and enchanted so many
thousands, accompanied Clara Schumann, and
the composer and the poet were alone the audience :
a little festive supper and a mutual interchange
of ideas shortened the evening only too much. I
met with the old, cordial reception at the house
of Mr. Brockhaus, to which from former visits I
had almost accustomed myself. The circle of my
friends increased in the German cities ; but the
first heart is still that to which we most gladly
turn again.

I found in Dresden old friends with youthful feelings ; my gifted half-countryman Dahl, the Norwegian, who knows how upon canvas to make the waterfall rush foaming down, and the birch-tree to grow as in the valleys of Norway, and Vogel von Vogelstein, who did me the honour of painting my portrait, which was included in the royal collection of portraits. The theatre intendant, Herr von Lüttichau, provided me every evening with a seat in the manager's box ; and one of the noblest ladies, in the first circles of Dresden, the worthy Baroness von Decken, received me as a mother would receive her son. In this character I was ever afterwards received in her family and in the amiable circle of her friends.

How bright and beautiful is the world ! How good are human beings ! That it is a pleasure to live becomes ever more and more clear to me.

Beaulieu's younger brother Edmund, who is an officer in the army, came one day from Tharand, where he had spent the summer months. I accompanied him to various places, spent some happy days among the pleasant scenery of the hills, and was received at the same time into various families.

I visited with the Baroness Decken, for the

first time, the celebrated and clever painter Retsch, who has published the bold outlines of Goethe, Shakspeare, &c. He lives a sort of Arcadian life among lowly vineyards on the way to Meissen. Every year he makes a present to his wife, on her birthday, of a new drawing, and always one of his best; the collection has grown through a course of years to a valuable album, which she, if he die before her, is to publish. Among the many glorious ideas there, one struck me as peculiar; the Flight into Egypt. It is night; every one sleeps in the picture,—Mary, Joseph, the flowers and the shrubs, nay even the ass which carries her —all, except the child Jesus, who, with open round countenance, watches over and illumines all. I related one of my stories to him, and for this I received a lovely drawing,—a beautiful young girl hiding herself behind the mask of an old woman; thus should the eternally youthful soul, with its blooming loveliness, peep forth from behind the old mask of the fairy-tale. Retsch's pictures are rich in thought, full of beauty, and a genial spirit.

I enjoyed the country-life of Germany with Major Serre and his amiable wife at their splendid residence of Maren ; it is not possible for any one to exercise greater hospitality than is done by these two kind-hearted people. A circle of intelligent, interesting individuals, were here assembled ; I remained among them above eight days, and there became acquainted with Kohl the traveller, and the clever authoress, the Countess Hahn-Hahn, in whom I discerned a woman by disposition and individual character in whom confidence may be placed. Where one is well received there one gladly lingers. I found myself unspeakably happy on this little journey in Germany, and became convinced that I was there no stranger. It was heart and truth to nature which people valued in my writings ; and, however excellent and praiseworthy the exterior beauty may be, however imposing the maxims of this world's wisdom, still it is heart and nature which have least changed by time, and which every body is best able to understand.

I returned home by way of Berlin, where I had not been for several years ; but the dearest of my friends there—Chamisso, was dead.

The fair wild swan which flew far o'er the earth,
And laid its head upon a wild swan's breast,

was now flown to a more glorious hemisphere ; I saw his children, who were now fatherless and motherless. From the young who here surround me, I discover that I am grown older ; I feel it not in myself. Chamisso's sons, whom I saw the last time playing here in the little garden with bare necks, came now to meet me with helmet and sword : they were officers in the Prussian service. I felt in a moment how the years had rolled on, how every thing was changed and how one loses so many.

> Yet is it not so hard as people deem,
> To see their souls beloved from them riven;
> God has their dear ones, and in death they seem
> To form a bridge which leads them up to heaven.

I met with the most cordial reception, and have since then always met with the same, in the house of the Minister Savigny, where I became acquainted with the clever, singularly gifted Bettina and her lovely spiritual-minded daughter. One hour's conversation with Bettina, during which she was the chief speaker, was so rich and full of interest, that I was almost rendered dumb by all this eloquence, this firework of wit. The world knows her writings, but another talent which she is possessed of, is less generally known, namely her talent for drawing. Here again it is the ideas which astonish us. It was thus, I observed, she had treated in a sketch an accident which had occurred just before, a young man being killed by the fumes of wine. You saw him descending half-naked into the cellar, round which lay the wine casks like monsters: Bacchanals and Bacchantes danced towards him, seized their victim and destroyed him! I know that Thorwaldsen, to whom she once showed all her drawings, was in the highest degree astonished by the ideas they contained.

It does the heart such good when abroad to find a house, where, when immediately you enter, eyes flash like festal lamps, a house where you can take peeps into a quiet, happy domestic life— such a house is that of Professor Weiss. Yet how many new acquaintance which were found, and old acquaintance which were renewed, ought I not to mention! I met Cornelius from Rome, Schelling from Munich, my countryman I might almost call him; Steffens, the Norwegian, and once again Tieck, whom I had not seen since my first visit to Germany. He was very much altered, yet his gentle, wise eyes were the same, the shake of his hand was the same. I felt that he loved me and wished me well. I must visit him in Potsdam, where he lived in ease and comfort. At dinner I became acquainted with his brother the sculptor.

From Tieck I learnt how kindly the King and Queen of Prussia were disposed towards me; that they had read my romance of Only a Fiddler, and inquired from Tieck about me. Meantime their Majesties were absent from Berlin. I had arrived the evening before their departure, when that abominable attempt was made upon their lives.

I returned to Copenhagen by Stettin in stormy weather, full of the joy of life, and again saw my dear friends, and in a few days set off to Count Moltke's in Funen, there to spend a few lovely summer days. I here received a letter from the minister Count Rantzau-Breitenburg, who was with the King and Queen of Denmark at the watering-place of Föhr. He wrote, saying that he had the pleasure of announcing to me the most gracious invitation of their Majesties to Föhr. This island, as is well known, lies in the North Sea, not far from the coast of Sleswick, in the neighbourhood of the interesting Halligs, those little islands which Biernatzky described so charmingly in his novels. Thus in a manner wholly unexpected by me, I should see scenery of a very peculiar character even in Denmark.

The favour of my King and Queen made me happy, and I rejoiced to be once more in close intimacy with Rantzau. Alas, it was for the last time!

It was just now five and twenty years since I, a poor lad, travelled alone and helpless to Copenhagen. Exactly the five and twentieth anniversary would be celebrated by my being with my King and Queen, to whom I was faithfully attached, and whom I at that very time learned to love with my whole soul. Every thing that surrounded me, man and nature, reflected themselves imperishably in my soul. I felt myself as it were, conducted to a joint from which I could look forth more distinctly over the past five and twenty years, with all the good fortune and happiness which they had evolved for me. The reality frequently surpasses the most beautiful dream.

I travelled from Funen to Flensborg, which, lying in its great bay, is picturesque with woods and hills, and then immediately opens out into a solitary heath. Over this I travelled in the bright moonlight. The journey across the heath was tedious ; the clouds only passed rapidly. We went on monotonously through the deep sand, and monotonous was the wail of a bird among the shrubby heath. Presently we reached moorlands. Long-continued rain had changed meadows and corn fields into great lakes ; the embankments along which we drove were like morasses ; the horses sank deeply into them. In many places the light carriage was obliged to be supported by the peasants, that it might not fall upon the cottages below the embankment. Several hours were consumed over each mile (Danish). At length the North Sea with its islands lay before me. The whole coast was an embankment, covered for miles with woven straw, against which the waves broke. I arrived at high tide. The wind was favourable, and in less than an hour I reached Föhr, which, after my difficult journey, appeared to me like a real fairyland.

The largest city, Wyck, in which are the baths, is exactly built like a Dutch town. The houses are only one story high, with sloping roofs and gables turned to the street. The many strangers there, and the presence of the court, gave a peculiar animation to the principal street. Well-known faces looked out from almost every house; the Danish flag waved, and music was heard. I was soon established in my quarters, and every day, until the departure of their majesties, had I the honour of an invitation from them to dinner, as well as to pass the evening in their circle. On several evenings I read aloud my little stories (Märchen) to the king and queen, and both of them were gracious and affectionate towards me. It is so good when a noble human nature will reveal itself where otherwise only the king's crown and the purple mantle might be discovered. Few people can be more amiable in private life than their present Majesties of Denmark. May God bless them and give them joy, even as they filled my breast with happiness and sunshine!

I sailed in their train to the largest of the Halligs, those grassy dunes in the ocean, which bear testimony to a sunken country. The violence of the sea has changed the mainland into islands, has riven these again, and buried men and villages. Year after year are new portions rent away, and,

in half a century's time, there will be nothing
here but sea. The Halligs are now only low islets
covered with a dark turf, on which a few flocks
graze. When the sea rises these are driven into
the garrets of the houses, and the waves roll over
this little region, which is miles distant from the
shore. Oland, which we visited, contains a little
town. The houses stand closely side by side, as
if, in their sore need, they would all huddle together. They are all erected upon a platform,
and have little windows, as in the cabin of a ship.
There, in the little room, solitary through half the
year, sit the wife and her daughters spinning.
There, however, one always finds a little collection
of books.   I found books in Danish, German, and
Frieslandish. The people read and work, and the
sea rises round the houses, which lie like a wreck
in the ocean. Sometimes, in the night, a ship,
having mistaken the lights, drives on here and is
stranded.

In the year 1825, a tempestuous tide washed
away men and houses. The people sat for days
and nights half naked upon the roofs, till these
gave way ; nor from Föhr nor the mainland could
help be sent to them. The churchyard is half

washed away ; coffins and corpses were frequently exposed to view by the breakers ; it is an appalling sight. And yet the inhabitants of the Halligs are attached to their little home. They cannot remain on the mainland, but are driven thence by home sickness.

We found only one man upon the island, and he had only lately risen from a sick bed. The others were out on long voyages. We were received by girls and women. They had erected before the church a triumphal arch with flowers, which they had fetched from Föhr ; but it was so small, and low, that one was obliged to go round it ; nevertheless they showed by it their good will. The queen was deeply affected by their having cut down their only shrub, a rose bush, to lay over a marshy place which she would have to cross. The girls are pretty, and are dressed in a half Oriental fashion. The people trace their descent from Greeks. They wear their faces half concealed, and beneath the strips of linen which lie upon the head is placed a Greek fez, around which the hair is wound in plaits.

On our return, dinner was served on board the royal steamer ; and afterwards, as we sailed in a glorious sunset through this archipelago, the deck of the vessel was changed to a dancing room. Young and old danced ; servants flew hither and thither with refreshments ; sailors stood upon the paddle-boxes and took the soundings, and their deep-toned voices might be heard giving the depth of the water. The moon rose round and large, and the promontory of Amrom assumed the appearance of a snow-covered chain of Alps.

I visited afterwards these desolate sand hills ; the king went to shoot rabbits there. Many years ago a ship was wrecked here, on board of which were two rabbits, and from this pair Amrom is now stored with thousands of their descendants. At low tide the sea recedes wholly from between Amrom and Föhr, and then people drive across from one island to another ; but still the time must be well observed and the passage accurately known, or else, when the tide comes, he who crosses will be inevitably lost. It requires only a few minutes, and then where dry land was large ships may sail. We saw a whole row of wagons driving from Föhr to Amrom. Seen upon the white sand and against the blue horizon, they seemed to be twice as large as they really were.

All around were spread out, like a net, the sheets of water, as if they held firmly the extent of sand which belonged to the ocean and which would be soon overflowed by it. This promontory brings to one's memory the mounds of ashes at Vesuvius; for here one sinks at every step, the wiry moor-grass not being able to bind together the loose sand. The sun shone burningly hot between the white sand hills : it was like a journey through the deserts of Africa.

A peculiar kind of rose, and the heath were in flower, in the valleys between the hills ; in other places where there was no vegetation whatever ; nothing but the wet sand on which the waves had left their impress ; the sea had inscribed on its receding strange hieroglyphics. I gazed from one of the highest points over the North Sea ; it was ebb-tide ; the sea had retired above a mile ; the vessels lay like dead fishes upon the sand, and awaiting the returning tide. A few sailors had clambered down and moved about on the sandy ground like black points. Where the sea itself kept the white level sand in movement, a long bank elevated itself, which, during the time of high-water, is concealed, and upon which occur many wrecks. I saw the lofty wooden tower which is here erected, and in which a cask is always kept filled with water, and a basket supplied with bread and brandy, that the unfortunate human beings, who are here stranded may be able in this place, amid the swelling sea, to preserve life for a few days until it is possible to rescue them.

To return from such a scene as this to a royal table, a charming court-concert, and a little ball in a bath-saloon, as well to the promenade by moonlight, thronged with guests, a little Boulevard, had something in it like a fairy tale,—it was a singular contrast.

As I sat on the above-mentioned five-and-twentieth anniversary, on the 5th of September, at the royal dinner-table, the whole of my former life passed in review before my mind. I was obliged to summon all my strength to prevent myself bursting into tears. There are moments of thankfulness in which, as it were, we feel a desire to press God to our hearts. How deeply, I felt, at this time, my own nothingness ; how all, had come from him. Rantzau knew what an interesting day this was to me. After dinner the king and the queen wished me happiness, and that so—*graciously*, is a poor word,—so cordially, so sympathisingly ! The king wished me happiness in that which I had endured and won. He asked me about my first entrance into the world, and I related to him some characteristic traits.

In the course of conversation he inquired if I had not some certain yearly income : I named the sum to him.

" That is not much," said the king.

" But I do not require much," replied I, " and my writings procure me something."

The king, in the kindest manner, inquired farther into my circumstances, and closed by saying.

" If I can in any way be serviceable to your literary labours, then come to me."

In the evening during the concert, the conversation was renewed, and some of those who stood near me reproached me for not having made use of my opportunity.

" The king," said they, " put the very words into your mouth."

But I could not, I would not have done it. " If the king," I said, " found that I required something more, he could give it to me of his own will."

And I was not mistaken. In the following year

King Christian VIII. increased my annual stipend, so that with this and that which my writings bring in, I can live honourably and free from care. My King gave it to me out of the pure good-will of his own heart. King Christian is enlightened, clear-sighted, with a mind enlarged by science ; the gracious sympathy, therefore, which he has felt in my fate is to me doubly cheering and ennobling.

The 5th of September was to me a festival day : even the German visitors at the baths honoured me by drinking my health in the pump-room.

So many flattering circumstances, some people argue, may easily spoil a man, and make him vain. But, no ; they do not spoil him, they make him on the contrary—better ; they purify his mind, and he must thereby feel an impulse, a wish, to deserve all that he enjoys. At my parting-audience with the queen, she gave me a valuable ring as a remembrance of our residence at Föhr ; and the king again expressed himself full of kindness and noble sympathy. God bless and preserve this exalted pair !

The Duchess of Augustenburg was at this time also at Föhr with her two eldest daughters. I had daily the happiness of being with them, and received repeated invitations to take Augustenburg on my return. For this purpose I went from Föhr to Als, one of the most beautiful islands in the Baltic. That little region resembles a blooming garden ; luxuriant corn and clover-fields are inclosed, with hedges of hazels and wild roses ; the peasants' houses are surrounded by large apple-orchards, full of fruit. Wood and hill alternate. Now we see the ocean, and now the narrow Lesser Belt, which resembles a river. The Castle of Augustenburg is magnificent, with its garden full of flowers, extending down to the very shores of the serpentine bay. I met with the most cordial reception and found the most amiable family-life in the ducal circle. I spent fourteen days here, and was present at the birthday festivities of the duchess, which lasted three days ; among these festivities was racing, and the town and the castle were filled with people.

Happy domestic life is like a beautiful summer's evening ; the heart is filled with peace ; and every thing around derives a peculiar glory. The full heart says " it is good to be here ; " and this I felt at Augustenburg.

CHAPTER VIII

IN the spring of 1844 I had finished a dramatic tale, " The Flower of Fortune." The idea of this was, that it is not the immortal name of the artist, nor the splendour of a crown which can make man happy ; but that happiness is to be found where people satisfied with little, love and are loved again. The scene was perfectly Danish, an idyllian, sunbright life, in whose clear heaven two dark pictures are reflected as in a dream : the unfortunate Danish poet Ewald and Prince Buris, who is tragically sung of in our heroic ballads. I wished to show, in honour of our times, the middle ages to have been dark and miserable, as they were, but which many poets only represent to us in a beautiful light.

Professor Heiberg, who was appointed censor, declared himself against the reception of my piece. During the last years I had met with nothing but hostility from this party : I regarded it as personal

THE COLLIN HOME
From a Painting by A. Petzholdt, about 1835

ill-will, and this was to me still more painful than
the rejection of the pieces. It was painful for me
to be placed in a constrained position with regard
to a poet whom I respected, and towards whom,
according to my own conviction, I had done every
thing in order to obtain a friendly relationship. A
further attempt, however, must be made. I wrote
to Heiberg, expressed myself candidly, and, as I
thought, cordially, and entreated him to give me
explicitly the reasons for his rejection of the piece
and for his ill-will towards me. He immediately
paid me a visit, which I, not being at home when
he called, returned on the following day, and I
was received in the most friendly manner. The
visit and the conversation belong certainly to
the extraordinary, but they occasioned an explanation, and I hope led to a better understanding for
the future.

He clearly set before me his views in the rejection of my piece. Seen from his point of sight
they were unquestionably correct ; but they were
not mine, and thus we could not agree. He
declared decidedly that he cherished no spite
against me, and that he acknowledged my talent.
I mentioned his various attacks upon me, for

example, in the Intelligence, and that he had denied to me original invention ; I imagined however, that I had shown this in my novels : " But of these," said I, " you have read none ; you yourself have told me so."

" Yes, that is the truth," replied he ; " I have not read them, but I will do so."

" Since then," continued I, " you have turned me and my Bazaar to ridicule in your poem called Denmark, and spoken about my fanaticism for the beautiful Dardanelles ; and yet I have, precisely in that book, described the Dardanelles as not beautiful ; it is the Bosphorus which I thought beautiful ; you seem not to be aware of that ; perhaps you have not read The Bazaar either ! "

" Was it the Bosphorus ! " said he, with his own peculiar smile ; " yes, I had quite forgotten that, and, you see, people do not remember it either ; the object in this case was only to give you a stab."

This confession sounded so natural, so like him, that I was obliged to smile. I looked into his clever eyes, thought how many beautiful things he had written, and I could not be angry with him.

The conversation became more lively, more free, and he said many kind things to me ; for example, he esteemed my stories very highly, and entreated me frequently to visit him. I have become more and more acquainted with his poetical temperament, and I fancy that he too will understand mine. We are very dissimilar, but we both strive after the same object. Before we separated he conducted me to his little observatory ; now his dearest world. He seems now to live for poetry and now for philosophy, and—for which I fancy he is least of all calculated—for astronomy. I could almost sigh and sing,

Thou wast erewhile the star at which thou gazest now !

My dramatic story came at length on the stage, and in the course of the season was performed seven times.

As people grow older, however much they may be tossed about in the world, some one place must be the true home; even the bird of passage has one fixed spot to which it hastens : mine was and is the house of my friend Collin. Treated as a son, almost grown up with the children, I have become a member of the family ; a more heartfelt connection, a better home have I never known :

a link broke in this chain, and precisely in the hour of bereavement, did I feel how firmly I have been engrafted here, so that I was regarded as one of the children.

If I were to give the picture of the mistress of a family who wholly loses her own individual I in her husband and children, I must name the wife of Collin ; with the sympathy of a mother, she also followed me in sorrow and in gladness. In the latter years of her life she became very deaf, and besides this she had the misfortune of being nearly blind. An operation was performed on her sight, which succeeded so well, that in the course of the winter she was able to read a letter, and this was a cause of grateful joy to her. She longed in an extraordinary manner for the first green of spring, and this she saw in her little garden.

I parted from her one Sunday evening in health and joy ; in the night I was awoke ; a servant brought me a letter. Collin wrote, "My wife is very ill ; the children are all assembled here ! " I understood it, and hastened thither. She slept quietly and without pain ; it was the sleep of the just ; it was death which was approaching so kindly and calmly. On the third day she yet lay in that peaceful slumber : then her countenance grew pale—and she was dead !

> Thou did'st but close thine eyes to gather in
> The large amount of all thy spiritual bliss;
> We saw thy slumbers like a little child's.
> O death ! thou art all brightness and not shadow.

Never had I imagined that the departure from this world could be so painless, so blessed. A devotion arose in my soul ; a conviction of God and eternity, which this moment elevated to an epoch in my life. It was the first deathbed at which I had been present since my childhood. Children, and children's children were assembled. In such moments all is holy around us. Her soul was love ; she went to love and to God !

At the end of July the monument of King Frederick VI. was to be uncovered at Skanderburg, in the middle of Jutland. I had, by solicitation written the cantata for the festival, to which Hartmann had furnished the music, and this was to be sung by Danish students. I had been invited to the festival, which thus was to form the object of my summer excursions.

Skanderburg lies in one of the most beautiful districts of Denmark. Agreeable hills rise covered

with vast beech-woods, and a large inland lake
of a pleasing form extends among them. On the
outside of the city, close by the church, which is
built upon the ruins of an old castle, now stands
the monument, a work of Thorwaldsen's. The
most beautiful moment to me at this festival was
in the evening, after the unveiling of the monument ; torches were lighted around it, and threw
their unsteady flame over the lake ; within the
woods blazed thousands of lights, and music for
the dance resounded from the tents. Round
about upon the hills, between the woods, and high
above them, bonfires were lighted at one end and
the same moment, which burned in the night like
red stars. There was spread over lake and land
a pure, a summer fragrance which is peculiar to
the north, in its beautiful summer nights. The
shadows of those who passed between the monument and the church, glided gigantically along
its red walls, as if they were spirits who were taking
part in the festival.

I returned home. In this year my novel of
the Improvisatore was translated into English,
by the well-known authoress, Mary Howitt, and
was received by her countrymen with great

applause. O. T. and the Fiddler soon followed, and met with, as it seemed, the same reception. After that appeared, a Dutch, and lastly a Russian translation of the Improvisatore. That which I should never have ventured to have dreamed of was accomplished ; my writings seem to come forth under a lucky star ; they fly over all lands. There is a something elevating, but at the same time, a something terrific in seeing one's thoughts spread so far, and among so many people ; it is indeed, almost a fearful thing to belong to so many. The noble and the good in us becomes a blessing ; but the bad, one's errors, shoot forth also, and involuntarily the thought forces itself from us : God ! let me never write down a word of which I shall not be able to give an account to thee. A peculiar feeling, a mixture of joy and anxiety, fills my heart every time my good genius conveys my fictions to a foreign people.

Travelling operates like an invigorating bath to the mind ; like a Medea-draft which always makes young again. I feel once more an impulse for it—not in order to seek up material, as a critic fancied and said, in speaking of my Bazaar ; there exists a treasury of material in my own inner self, and this life is too short to mature this young existence ; but there needs refreshment of spirit in order to convey it vigorously and maturely to paper, and travelling is to me, as I have said, this invigorating bath, from which I return as it were younger and stronger.

By prudent economy, and the proceeds of my writings, I was in a condition to undertake several journeys during the last year. That which for me is the most sunbright, is the one in which these pages were written. Esteem, perhaps, over-estimation, but especially kindness, in short, happiness and pleasure have flowed towards me in abundant measure.

I wished to visit Italy for the third time, there to spend a summer, that I might become acquainted with the south in its warm season, and probably return thence by Spain and France. At the end of October, 1845, I left Copenhagen. Formerly I had thought when I set out on a journey, God! what wilt thou permit to happen to me on this journey ! This time my thoughts were, God, what will happen to my friends at home during this long time ! And I felt a real anxiety. In one year the hearse may drive up to the door many times, and whose name may shine upon the coffin ! The proverb says, when one suddenly feels a cold shudder " now death passes over my grave." The shudder is still colder when the thoughts pass over the graves of our best friends.

I spent a few days at Count Moltke's, at Glorup ; strolling players were acting some of my dramatic works at one of the nearest provincial towns. I did not see them ; country life firmly withheld me. There is something in the late autumn poetically beautiful ; when the leaf is fallen from the tree, and the sun shines still upon the green grass, and the bird twitters, one may often fancy that it is a spring-day ; thus certainly also has the old man moments in his autumn in which his heart dreams of spring.

I passed only one day in Odense—I feel myself there more of a stranger than in the great cities of Germany. As a child I was solitary, and had therefore no youthful friend ; most of the families whom I knew have died out ; a new generation passes along the streets ; and the streets even are altered. The later buried have concealed the miserable graves of my parents. Every thing is changed. I took one of my childhood's rambles to the Marianheights which have belonged to the Iversen family ; but this family is dispersed ; unknown faces looked out from the windows. How many youthful thoughts have been here exchanged !

One of the young girls who at that time sat quietly there with beaming eyes and listened to my first poem, when I came here in the summer time as a scholar from Slagelse, sits now far quieter in noisy Copenhagen, and has thence sent out her first writings into the world. Her German publisher thought that some introductory words from me might be useful to them, and I, the stranger, but the almost too kindly received, have introduced the works of this clever girl into Germany.

It is Henrietta Hanck of whom I speak, the authoress of "Aunt Anna," and "An Author's Daughter."* I visited her birth-place when the first little circle paid me homage and gave me joy. But all was strange there, I myself a stranger.

---

* Since these pages were written, I have received from home the news of her death, in July, 1846. She was an affectionate daughter to her parents, and was besides this, possessed of a deeply poetical mind. In her I have lost a true friend from the years of childhood, one who had felt an interest and a sisterly regard for me, both in my good and my evil days.

The ducal family of Augustenburg was now
at Castle Gravenstein ; they were informed of my
arrival, and all the favour and the kindness which
was shown to me on the former occasion at Augustenburg was here renewed in rich abundance. I
remained here fourteen days, and it was as if these
were an announcement of all the happiness which
should meet me when I arrived in Germany. The
country around here is of the most picturesque
description ; vast woods, cultivated uplands in
perpetual variety, with the winding shore of the
bay and the many quiet inland lakes. Even the
floating mists of autumn lent to the landscape a
somewhat picturesque, something strange to the
islander. Every thing here is on a larger scale
than on the island. Beautiful was it without,
glorious was it within. I wrote here a new little
story—The Girl with the Brimstone matches ;
the only thing which I wrote upon this journey.
Receiving the invitation to come often to Gravenstein and Augustenburg, I left, with a grateful
heart, a place where I had spent such beautiful
and such happy days.

Now, no longer the traveller goes at a snail's
pace through the deep sand over the heath ; the

railroad conveys him in a few hours to Altona
and Hamburg. The circle of my friends there is
increased within the last years. The greater
part of my time I spent with my oldest friends
Count Holk, and the resident Minister Bille, and
with Zeise, the excellent translator of my stories.
Otto Speckter, who is full of genius, surprised me
by his bold, glorious drawings for my stories ;
he had made a whole collection of them, six only
of which were known to me. The same natural
freshness which shows itself in every one of his
works and makes them all little works of art,
exhibits itself in his whole character. He appears
to possess a patriarchal family, an affectionate old
father, and gifted sisters, who love him with their
whole souls. I wished one evening to go to the
theatre : it was scarcely a quarter of an hour before
the commencement of the opera : Speckter accompanied me, and on our way we came up to an
elegant house.

" We must first go in here, dear friend," said
he ; " a wealthy family lives here, friends of mine,
and friends of your stories ; the children will be
happy."

" But the opera," said I.

" Only for two minutes," returned he ; and drew me into the house, mentioned my name and the circle of children collected around me.

" And now tell us a tale," said he ; " only one."

I told one, and then hastened away to the theatre.

" That was an extraordinary visit," said I.

" An excellent one ; one entirely out of the common way ; one entirely out of the common way ! " said he exultingly ; " only think ; the children are full of Andersen and his stories ; he suddenly makes his appearance amongst them, tells one of them himself, and then is gone ! vanished ! That is of itself like a fairy-tale to the children, that will remain vividly in their remembrance."

I myself was amused by it.

In Oldenburg my own little room, home-like and comfortable, was awaiting me. Hofrath von Eisendecker and his well-informed lady whom, among all my foreign friends I may consider as my most sympathising, expected me. I had promised to remain with them a fortnight, but I stayed much longer. A house where the best and the most intellectual people of a city meet, is an

agreeable place of residence, and such a one had
I here. A deal of social intercourse prevailed in
the little city, and the theatre, in which certainly
either opera or ballet was given, is one of the most
excellent in Germany. The ability of Gall, the
director, is sufficiently known, and unquestionably
the nomination of the poet Mosen has a great and
good influence. I have to thank him for enabling
me to see one of the classic pieces of Germany,
Nathan the Wise, the principal part in which was
played by Kaiser, who is as remarkable for his
deeply studied and excellent tragic acting, as for
his readings.

Mosen, who somewhat resembles Alexander
Dumas, with his half African countenance, and
brown sparkling eyes, although he was suffering
in body, was full of life and soul, and we soon
understood one another. A trait of his little son
affected me. He had listened to me with great
devotion, as I read one of my stories ; and when
on the last day I was there, I took leave, the mother
said that he must give me his hand, adding, that
probably a long time must pass before he would
see me again, the boy burst into tears. In the
evening, when Mosen came into the theatre, he

said to me, " My little Erick has two tin soldiers ;
one of them he has given me for you, that you
may take him with you on your journey."

The tin soldier has faithfully accompanied me ;
he is a Turk : probably some day he may relate
his travels.

Mosen wrote in the dedication of his " John
of Austria," the following lines to me :—

> Once a little bird flew over
> From the North Sea's dreary strand ;
> Singing, flew unto me over,
> Singing Märchen through the land.
> Farewell ! Yet again bring hither
> Thy warm heart and song together.

Here I again met with Mayer, who has described
Naples and the Neapolitans so charmingly. My
little stories interested him so much that he had
written a little treatise on them for Germany.
Kapellmeister Pott, and my countryman Jerndorff,
belong to my earlier friends. I made every day
new acquaintance, because all houses were open
to me through the family with whom I was staying.
Even the Grand Duke was so generous as to have
me invited to a concert at the palace the day after
my arrival, and later I had the honour of being
asked to dinner. I received in this foreign court,

especially, many unlooked-for favours. At the Eisendeckers and at the house of the parents of my friend Beaulieu—the Privy-Counsellor Beaulieu, at Oldenburg, I heard several times my little stories read in German.

I can read Danish very well, as it ought to be read, and I can give to it perfectly the expression which ought to be given in reading : there is in the Danish language a power which cannot be transfused into a translation ; the Danish language is peculiarly excellent for this species of fiction. The stories have a something strange to me in German ; it is difficult for me in reading it to put my Danish soul into it ; my pronunciation of the German also is feeble, and with particular words I must, as it were, use an effort to bring them out—and yet people everywhere in Germany have had great interest in hearing me read them aloud. I can very well believe that the foreign pronunciation in the reading of these tales may be easily permitted, because this foreign manner approaches, in this instance, to the childlike ; it gives a natural colouring to the reading. I saw everywhere that the most distinguished men and women of the most highly cultivated minds, listened to me with

interest ; people entreated me to read, and I did
so willingly. I read for the first time my stories
in a foreign tongue, and at a foreign court, before
the Grand Duke of Oldenburg and a little select
circle.

The winter soon came on ; the meadows which
lay under water, and which formed large lakes
around the city, were already covered with thick
ice ; the skaters flew over it, and I yet remained in
Oldenburg among my hospitable friends. Days
and evenings slid rapidly away; Christmas approached, and this season I wished to spend in
Berlin. But what are distances in our days ?—
the steam-carriage goes from Hanover to Berlin
in one day ! I must away from the beloved ones,
from children and old people, who were near, as it
were, to my heart.

I was astonished in the highest degree on taking
leave of the Grand Duke, to receive from him, as a
mark of his favour and as a keepsake, a valuable
ring. I shall always preserve it, like every other
remembrance of this country, where I have found
and where I possess true friends.

When I was in Berlin on the former occasion,
I was invited, as the author of the Improvisatore,

to the Italian Society, into which only those who have visited Italy can be admitted. Here I saw Rauch for the first time, who, with his white hair and his powerful manly figure, is not unlike Thorwaldsen. Nobody introduced me to him, and I did not venture to present myself, and therefore walked alone about his studio like the other strangers. Afterwards I became personally acquainted with him at the house of the Prussian Ambassador, in Copenhagen ; I now hastened to him.

He was in the highest degree captivated by my little stories, pressed me to his breast, and expressed the highest praise, but which was honestly meant. Such a momentary estimation or over-estimation from a man of genius erases many a dark shadow from the mind. I received from Rauch my first welcome in Berlin : he told me what a large circle of friends I had in the capital of Prussia. I must acknowledge that it was so. They were of the noblest in mind as well as the first in rank, in art, and in science. Alexander von Humboldt, Prince Radziwil, Savigny, and many others never to be forgotten.

I had already, on the former occasion, visited

the brothers Grimm, but I had not at that time
made much progress with the acquaintance. I
had not brought any letters of introduction to
them with me, because people had told me, and I
myself believed it, that if I were known by anybody in Berlin, it must be the brothers Grimm. I
therefore sought out their residence. The servant-
maid asked me with which of the brothers I wished
to speak.

"With the one who has written the most," said
I, because I did not know, at that time, which of
them had most interested himself in the Märchen.

"Jacob is the most learned," said the maid-
servant.

"Well, then, take me to him."

I entered the room, and Jacob Grimm, with
his knowing and strongly-marked countenance,
stood before me.

"I come to you," said I, "without letters of
introduction, because I hope that my name is not
wholly unknown to you."

"Who are you?" asked he.

"I told him, and Jacob Grimm said, in a half-
embarrassed voice, "I do not remember to have
heard this name; what have you written?"

It was now my turn to be embarrassed in a high degree : but I now mentioned my little stories.

" I do not know them," said he ; " but mention to me some other of your writings, because I certainly must have heard them spoken of."

I named the titles of several ; but he shook his head. I felt myself quite unlucky.

" But what must you think of me," said I, " that I come to you as a total stranger, and enumerate myself what I have written : you must know me ! There has been published in Denmark a collection of the Märchen of all nations, which is dedicated to you, and in it there is at least one story of mine."

" No," said he good-humouredly, but as much embarrassed as myself ; " I have not read even that, but it delights me to make your acquaintance ; allow me to conduct you to my brother Wilhelm ? "

" No, I thank you," said I, only wishing now to get away ; I had fared badly enough with one brother. I pressed his hand and hurried from the house.

That same month Jacob Grimm went to Copenhagen ; immediately on his arrival, and while yet in his travelling dress, did the amiable kind man hasten up to me. He now knew me, and he came to me with cordiality. I was just then standing and packing my clothes in a trunk for a journey to the country ; I had only a few minutes time : by this means my reception of him was just as laconic as had been his of me in Berlin.

Now, however, we met in Berlin as old acquaintance. Jacob Grimm is one of those characters whom one must love and attach oneself to.

One evening, as I was reading one of my little stories at the Countess Bismark-Bohlen's there was in the little circle one person in particular who listened with evident fellowship of feeling, and who expressed himself in a peculiar and sensible manner on the subject,—this was Jacob's brother, Wilhelm Grimm.

" I should have known you very well, if you had come to me," said he, " the last time you were here."

I saw these two highly gifted and amiable brothers almost daily ; the circles into which I was invited seemed also to be theirs, and it was my desire and pleasure that they should listen to my little stories, that they should participate in them, they whose name will be always spoken as long as the German *Volksmärchen* are read.

The fact of my not being known to Jacob Grimm on my first visit to Berlin had so disconcerted me, that when any one asked me whether I had been well received in this city, I shook my head doubtfully and said, " but Grimm did not know me."

I was told that Tieck was ill—could see no one ; I therefore only sent in my card. Some days afterwards I met at a friend's house, where Rauch's birth-day was being celebrated, Tieck, the sculptor, who told me that his brother had lately waited two hours for me at dinner. I went to him and discovered that he had sent me an invitation, which, however, had been taken to a wrong inn. A fresh invitation was given, and I passed some delightfully cheerful hours with Raumer the historian, and with the widow and daughter of Steffens. There is a music in Tieck's voice, a spirituality in his intelligent eyes, which age cannot lessen, but, on the contrary, must increase. The Elves, perhaps the most beautiful story which has been conceived in our time, would alone be sufficient, had Tieck written nothing else, to make his name immortal. As the author of *Märchen*, I bow myself before him, the elder and the master, and who was the first German poet, who many years before pressed me to his breast, as if it were to consecrate me, to walk in the same path with himself.

The old friends had all to be visited ; but the number of new ones grew with each day. One invitation followed another. It required considerable physical power to support so much goodwill. I remained in Berlin about three weeks, and the time seemed to pass more rapidly with each succeeding day. I was, as it were, overcome by kindness. I, at length, had no other prospect for repose than to seat myself in a railway-carriage, and fly away out of the country.

And yet amid these social festivities, with all the amiable zeal and interest that then was felt for me, I had one disengaged evening ; one evening on which I suddenly felt solitude in its most oppressive form ; Christmas-eve, that very evening of all others on which I would most willingly witness something festal, willingly stand beside a Christmas-tree, gladdening myself with the joy of children, and seeing the parents joyfully become children again. Every one of the many families in which I in truth felt that I was received as a relation, had fancied, as I afterwards discovered, that I must be invited out ; but I sat quite alone in my room at the inn, and thought on home. I seated myself at the open window, and gazed up to the starry heavens, which was the Christmas-tree that was lighted for me.

" Father in Heaven," I prayed, as the children do, " what dost thou give to me ! "

When the friends heard of my solitary Christmas night, there were on the following evening many Christmas-trees lighted, and on the last evening in the year, there was planted for me alone, a little tree with its lights, and its beautiful presents— and that was by Jenny Lind. The whole company consisted of herself, her attendant, and me ; we three children from the north were together on Sylvester-eve, and I was the child for which the Christmas-tree was lighted. She rejoiced with the feeling of a sister in my good fortune in Berlin ; and I felt almost pride in the sympathy of such a pure, noble, and womanly being. Everywhere her praise resounded, not merely as a singer, but also as a woman ; the two combined awoke a real enthusiasm for her.

It does one good both in mind and heart to see that which is glorious understood and beloved. In one little anecdote contributing to her triumph I was myself made the confident.

One morning I looked out of my window *unter den Linden*, I saw a man under one of the trees, half hidden, and shabbily dressed, who took a comb out of his pocket, smoothed his hair, set his neckerchief straight, and brushed his coat with his hand; I understood that bashful poverty which feels depressed by its shabby dress. A moment after this, there was a knock at my door, and this same man entered. It was W——, the poet of nature, who is only a poor tailor, but who has a truly poetical mind. Rellstab and others in Berlin have mentioned him with honour; there is something healthy in his poems, among which several of a sincerely religious character may be found. He had read that I was in Berlin, and wished now to visit me. We sat together on the sofa and conversed : there was such an amiable contentedness, such an unspoiled and good tone of mind, about him, that I was sorry not to be rich in order that I might do something for him. I was ashamed of offering him the little that I could give ; In any case I wished to put it in as agreeable a form as I could. I asked him whether I might invite him to hear Jenny Lind.

"I have already heard her," said he smiling ; "I had, it is true, no money to buy a ticket ; but I went to the leader of the supernumeraries, and asked whether I might not act as a supernumerary for one evening in Norma : I was accepted and habited as a Roman soldier, with a long sword by my side, and thus got to the theatre, where I could hear her better than any body else, for I stood close to her. Ah, how she sung, how she played ! I could not help crying ; but they were angry at that ; the leader forbade and would not let me again make my appearance, because no one must weep on the stage."

With the exception of the theatre, I had very little time to visit collections of any kind or institutions of art. The able and amiable Olfers, however, the Director of the Museum, enabled me to pay a rapid but extremely interesting visit to that institution. Olfers himself was my conductor ; we delayed our steps only for the most interesting objects, and there are here not few of these ; his remarks threw light upon my mind,—for this therefore I am infinitely obliged to him.

I had the happiness of visiting the Princess of Prussia many times; the wing of the castle in which she resided was so comfortable, and yet like a fairy palace. The blooming winter-garden, where the fountain splashed among the moss at the foot of the statue, was close beside the room in which the kind-hearted children smiled with their soft blue eyes. On taking leave she honoured me with a richly bound album, in which beneath the picture of the palace, she wrote her name. I shall guard this volume as a treasure of the soul; it is not the gift which has a value only, but also the manner in which it is given. One forenoon I read to her several of my little stories, and her noble husband listened kindly. Prince Pückler-Muskau also was present.

A few days after my arrival in Berlin, I had the honour to be invited to the royal table. As I was better acquainted with Humboldt than any one there, and he it was who had particularly interested himself about me, I took my place at his side. Not only on account of his high intellectual character, and his amiable and polite behaviour, but also from his infinite kindness towards me, during the whole of my residence in Berlin, is he become unchangeably dear to me.

The King received me most graciously, and said that during his stay in Copenhagen he had inquired after me, and had heard that I was travelling. He expressed a great interest in my novel of Only a Fiddler ; her Majesty the Queen also showed herself graciously and kindly disposed towards me. I had afterwards the happiness of being invited to spend an evening at the palace at Potsdam ; an evening which is full of rich remembrance and never to be forgotten ! Besides the ladies and gentlemen in waiting, Humboldt and myself were only invited. A seat was assigned to me at the table of their Majesties, exactly the place, said the Queen, where Oehlenschläger had sat and read his tragedy of Dina. I read four little stories, The Fir-Tree, The Ugly Duckling, The Ball and the Top, and The Swineherd. The King listened with great interest, and expressed himself most wittily on the subject. He said, how beautiful he thought the natural scenery of Denmark, and how excellently he had seen one of Holberg's comedies performed.

It was so deliciously pleasant in the royal apartment,—gentle eyes were gazing at me, and I felt that they all wished me well. When at night I was alone in my chamber, my thoughts were so occupied with this evening, and my mind in such a state of excitement, that I could not sleep. Every thing seemed to me like a fairy tale. Through the whole night the chimes sounded in the tower, and the aërial music mingled itself with my thoughts.

I received still one more proof of my favour and kindness of the King of Prussia towards me, on the evening before my departure from the city. The order of the Red Eagle, of the third class, was conferred upon me. Such a mark of honour delights certainly every one who receives it. I confess candidly that I felt myself honoured in a high degree. I discerned in it an evident token of the kindness of the noble, enlightened King towards me : my heart is filled with gratitude. I received this mark of honour exactly on the birthday of my benefactor Collin, the 6th of January ; this day has now a twofold festal significance for me. May God fill with gladness the mind of the royal donor who wished to give me pleasure !

The last evening was spent in a warm-hearted circle, for the greater part, of young people. My health was drunk; a poem, Der Märchenkönig, declaimed. It was not until late in the night that I reached home, that I might set off early in the morning by railroad.

I have here given in part a proof of the favour and kindness which was shown to me in Berlin: I feel like some one who has received a considerable sum for a certain object from a large assembly, and now would give an account thereof. I might still add many other names, as well from the learned world, as Theodor Mügge, Geibel, Häring, etc., as from the social circle,—the reckoning is too large. God give me strength for that which I now have to perform, after I have, as an earnest of goodwill, received such a richly abundant sum.

After a journey of a day and a night I was once more in Weimar, with my noble Hereditary Grand Duke. What a cordial reception! A heart rich in goodness, and a mind full of noble endeavours, live in this young prince. I have no words for the infinite favour, which, during my residence here, I received daily from the family of the Grand Duke, but my whole heart is full of devotion. At the court festival, as well as in the familiar family circle. I had many evidences of the esteem in which I was held. Beaulieu cared for me with the tenderness of a brother. It was to me a month-long Sabbath festival. Never shall I forget the quiet evenings spent with him, when friend spoke freely to friend.

My old friends were also unchanged; the wise and able Schöll, as well as Schober, joined them also. Jenny Lind came to Weimar; I heard her at the court concerts and at the theatre; I visited with her the places which are become sacred through Goethe and Schiller: we stood together beside their coffins, where Chancellor von Müller led us. The Austrian poet, Rollet, who met us here for the first time, wrote on this subject a sweet poem, which will serve me as a visible remembrance of this hour and this place. People lay lovely flowers in their books, and as such, I lay in here this verse of this:—

Weimar, 29th January, 1846.

Märchen rose, which hast so often
    Charm'd me with thy fragrant breath;
Where the prince, the poets slumber,
    Thou hast wreath'd the hall of death.

And with thee beside each coffin,
    In the death-hush'd chamber pale,
I beheld a grief-enchanted,
    Sweetly dreaming nightingale.

I rejoic'd amid the stillness;
    Gladness through my bosom past,
That the gloomy poet's coffins
    Such a magic crown d at last.

And thy rose's summer fragrance.
    Floated round that chamber pale,
With the gentle melancholy
    Of the grief-hush'd nightingale.

It was in the evening circle of the intellectual
Froriep that I met for the first time, with Auerbach,
who then chanced to be staying in Weimar. His
"Village Tales" interested me in the highest
degree; I regard them as the most poetical, most
healthy, and joyous production of the young
German literature. He himself made the same
agreeable impression upon me; there is something
so frank and straightforward, and yet so sagacious,
in his whole appearance, I might also say that he
looks himself like a village tale, healthy to the
core, body and soul, and his eyes beaming with
honesty. We soon became friends—and I hope
for ever.

My stay in Weimar was prolonged; it became

ever more difficult to tear myself away. The Grand Duke's birthday occurred at this time, and after attending all the festivities to which I was invited, I departed. I would and must be in Rome at Easter. Once more in the early morning, I saw the Hereditary Grand Duke, and, with a heart full of emotion, bade him farewell. Never, in presence of the world, will I forget the high position which his birth gives him, but I may say, as the very poorest subject may say of a prince, I love him as one who is dearest to my heart. God give him joy and bless him in his noble endeavours ! A generous heart beats beneath the princely star.

Beaulieu accompanied me to Jena. Here a hospitable home awaited me, and filled with beautiful memories from the time of Goethe, the house of the publisher Frommann. It was his kind, warm-hearted sister, who had shown me such sympathy in Berlin ; the brother was not here less kind.

The Holstener Michelsen, who has a professorship at Jena, assembled a number of friends one evening, and in a graceful and cordial toast for me expressed his sense of the importance of Danish literature, and the healthy and natural spirit which flourished in it.

In Michelsen's house I also became acquainted with Professor Hase, who, one evening having heard some of my little stories, seemed filled with great kindness towards me. What he wrote in this moment of interest on an album leaf expresses this sentiment :

" Schelling—not he who now lives in Berlin, but he who lives an immortal hero in the world of mind—once said : ' Nature is the visible spirit.' This spirit, this unseen nature, last evening was again rendered visible to me through your little tales. If on the one hand you penetrate deeply into the mysteries of nature ; know and understand the language of birds, and what are the feelings of a fir-tree or a daisy, so that each seems to be there on its own account, and we and our children sympathise with them in their joys and sorrows ; yet, on the other hand, all is but the image of mind ; and the human heart in its infinity, trembles and throbs throughout. May this fountain in the poet's heart, which God has lent you, still for a time pour forth this refreshingly, and may these stories in the memories of the Germanic nations become the legions of the people ! " That object, for which as a writer of poetical fictions, I must strive after, is contained in these last lines.

It is also to Hase and the gifted improvisatore, Professor Wolff of Jena, to whom I am most indebted for the appearance of a uniform German edition of my writings.

This was all arranged on my arrival at Leipzig : several hours of business were added to my traveller's mode of life. The city of book-selling presented me with her bouquet, a sum of money ; but she presented me with even more. I met again with Brockhaus, and passed happy hours with Mendelssohn, that glorious man of genius. I heard him play again and again ; it seemed to me that his eyes, full of soul, looked into the very depths of my being. Few men have more the stamp of the inward fire than he. A gentle, friendly wife, and beautiful children, make his rich, well-appointed house, blessed and pleasant. When he rallied me about the Stork, and its frequent appearance in my writings, there was something so childlike and amiable revealed in this great artist !

I also met again my excellent countryman

Gade, whose compositions have been so well received in Germany. I took him the text for a new opera which I had written, and which I hope to see brought out on the German stage. Gade had written the music to my drama of Agnete and the Merman, compositions which were very successful. Auerbach, whom I again found here, introduced me to many agreeable circles. I met with the composer Kalliwoda, and with Kühne, whose charming little son immediately won my heart.

On my arrival at Dresden I instantly hastened to my motherly friend, the Baroness von Decken. That was a joyous hearty welcome! One equally cordial I met with from Dahl. I saw once more my Roman friend, the poet with word and colour, Reineck, and met the kindhearted Bendemann. Professor Grahl painted me. I missed, however, one among my olden friends, the poet Brunnow. With life and cordiality he received me the last time in his room, where stood lovely flowers; now these grew over his grave. It awakens a peculiar feeling, thus for once to meet on the journey of life, to understand and love each other, and then to part—until the journey for both is ended.

I spent, to me a highly interesting evening, with the royal family, who received me with extraordinary favour. Here also the most happy domestic life appeared to reign—a number of amiable children, all belonging to Prince Johann, were present. The least of the Princesses, a little girl, who knew that I had written the history of the Fir-tree, began very confidentially with—"Last Christmas we also had a Fir-tree, and it stood here in this room!" Afterwards, when she was led out before the other children, and had bade her parents the king and queen good-night, she turned round at the half-closed door, and nodding to me in a friendly and familiar manner, said I was her Fairy-tale Prince.

My story of Holger Danske led the conversation to the rich stores of legends which the north possesses. I related several, and explained the peculiar spirit of the fine scenery of Denmark. Neither in this royal palace did I feel the weight of ceremony; soft, gentle eyes shone upon me. My last morning in Dresden was spent with the Minister von Könneritz, where I equally met with the most friendly reception.

The sun shone warm : it was spring who was

celebrating her arrival, as I rolled out of the dear
city.   Thought assembled in amount all the many
who had rendered my visits so rich and happy :
it was spring around me, and spring in my heart.

In Prague I had only one acquaintance, Professor
Wiesenfeldt. But a letter from Dr. Carus in
Dresden opened to me the hospitable house of
Count Thun. The Archduke Stephan received
me also in the most gracious manner ; I found in
him a young man full of intellect and heart.
Besides it was a very interesting point of time
when I left Prague. The military, who had been
stationed there a number of years, were hastening
to the railway, to leave for Poland, where disturb-
ances had broken out. The whole city seemed in
movement to take leave of its military friends ;
it was difficult to get through the streets which
led to the railway. Many thousand soldiers were
to be accommodated ; at length the train was set
in motion. All around the whole hill side was
covered with people ; it looked like the richest
Turkey carpet woven of men, women and children,
all pressed together, head to head, and waving
hats and handkerchiefs. Such a mass of human
beings I never saw before, or at least, never at one

moment surveyed them : such a spectacle could not be painted.

We travelled the whole night through wide Bohemia : at every town stood groups of people ; it was as though all the inhabitants had assembled themselves. Their brown faces, their ragged clothes, the light of their torches, their, to me, unintelligible language, gave to the whole a stamp of singularity. We flew through tunnel and over viaduct ; the windows rattled, the signal whistle sounded, the steam horses snorted—I laid back my head at last in the carriage, and fell asleep under the protection of the god Morpheus.

At Olmütz, where we had fresh carriages, a voice spoke my name—it was Walter Göethe ! We had travelled together the whole night without knowing it. In Vienna we met often. Noble powers, true genius, live in Goethe's grandsons, in the composer as well as in the poet ; but it is as if the greatness of their grandfather pressed upon me. Liszt was in Vienna, and invited me to his concert, in which otherwise it would have been impossible to find a place. I again heard his improvising of Robert ! I again heard him, like a spirit of the storm, play with the chords : he is an enchanter of sounds who fills the imagination with astonishment. Ernst also was here ; when I visited him he seized the violin, and this sang in tears the secret of a human heart.

I saw the amiable Grillparzer again, and was frequently with the kindly Castelli, who just at this time had been made by the King of Denmark Knight of the Danebrog Order. He was full of joy at this, and begged me to tell my countrymen that every Dane should receive a hearty welcome from him. Some future summer he invited me to visit his grand country seat. There is something in Castelli so open and honourable, mingled with such good-natured humour, that one must like him : he appears to me the picture of a thorough Viennese. Under his portrait, which he gave me, he wrote the following little improvised verse in the style so peculiarly his own :

This portrait shall ever with loving eyes greet thee,
    From far shall recall the smile of thy friend;
For thou, dearest Dane, 'tis a pleasure to meet thee,
    Thou art one to be lov'd and esteem'd to the end.

Castelli introduced me to Seidl and Bauernfeld. At the Danish Ambassador's, Baron von Löwenstern, I met Zedlitz. Most of the shining stars of

Austrian literature I saw glide past me, as people
on a railway see church towers ; you can still say
you have seen them ; and still retaining the simile
of the stars, I can say, that in the Concordia Society
I saw the entire galaxy. Here was a host of young
growing intellects, and here were men of importance. At the house of Count Szechenye, who
hospitably invited me, I saw his brother from
Pest, whose noble activity in Hungary is known.
This short meeting I account one of the most
interesting events of my stay in Vienna ; the man
revealed himself in all his individuality, and
his eye said that you must feel confidence in
him.

At my departure from Dresden her Majesty
the Queen of Saxony had asked me whether I
had introductions to any one at the Court of
Vienna, and when I told her that I had not, the
Queen was so gracious as to write a letter to her
sister, the Archduchess Sophia of Austria. Her
imperial Highness summoned me one evening,
and received me in the most gracious manner.
The dowager Empress, the widow of the Emperor
Francis I., was present, and full of kindness and
friendship towards me ; also Prince Wasa, and the

hereditary Archduchess of Hesse-Darmstadt. The remembrance of this evening will always remain dear and interesting to me. I read several of my little stories aloud—when I wrote them, I thought least of all that I should some day read them aloud in the imperial palace.

Before my departure I had still another visit to make, and this was to the intellectual authoress, Frau von Weissenthurn. She had just left a bed of sickness and was still suffering, but wished to see me. As though she were already standing on the threshold of the realm of shades, she pressed my hand and said this was the last time we should ever see each other. With a soft motherly gaze she looked at me, and at parting her penetrating eye followed me to the door.

With railway and diligence my route now led towards Trieste. With steam the long train of carriages flies along the narrow rocky way, following all the windings of the river. One wonders that with all these abrupt turnings one is not dashed against the rock or flung down into the roaring stream, and is glad when the journey is happily accomplished. But in the slow diligence one wishes its more rapid journey might recommence, and praise the powers of the age.

At length Trieste and the Adriatic Sea lay before us ; the Italian language sounded in our ears, but yet for me it was not Italy, the land of my desire. Meanwhile I was only a stranger here for a few hours ; our Danish consul, as well as the consuls of Prussia and Oldenburg, to whom I was recommended, received me in the best possible manner. Several interesting acquaintances were made, especially with the Counts O'Donnell and Waldstein, the latter for me as a Dane having a peculiar interest, as being the descendant of that unfortunate Corfitz Ulfeld and the daughter of Christian IV., Eleonore, the noblest of all Danish women. Their portraits hung in his room, and Danish memorials of that period were shown me. It was the first time I had ever seen Eleonore Corfitz Ulfeld's portrait, and the melancholy smile on her lips seemed to say, "Poet, sing and free from chains which a hard age had cast upon him, for whom to live and to suffer was my happiness ! " Before Oehlenschläger wrote his Dina, which treats of an episode in Corfitz Ulfeld's life, I was at work on this subject, and wished to bring it on the stage, but it was then feared this would not be allowed, and I gave it up—since then I have only written four lines on Corfitz Ulfeld :—

Thy virtue was conceal'd, not so thy failings,
Thus did the world thy greatness never know;
Yet still love's glorious monument proclaims it,
That the best wife from thee would never go.

On the Adriatic sea I, in thought, was carried back to Corfitz Ulfeld's time and the Danish Islands. This meeting with Count Waldstein and his ancestor's portrait brought me back to my poet's world and I almost forgot that the following day I could be in the middle of Italy. In beautiful mild weather I went with the steamboat to Ancona.

It was a quiet starlight night, too beautiful to be spent in sleep. In the early morning the coast of Italy lay before us, the beautiful blue mountains with glittering snow. The sun shone warmly, the grass and the trees were so splendidly green. Last evening in Trieste, now in Ancona, in a city of the papal states,—that was almost like enchantment ! Italy in all its picturesque splendour lay once more before me ; spring had ripened all the fruit trees so that they had burst forth into blossom ;

every blade of grass in the field was filled with sunshine, the elm trees stood like caryatides enwreathed with vines, which shot forth green leaves, and above the luxuriance of foliage rose the wavelike blue mountains with their snow covering. In company with Count Paar from Vienna, the most excellent travelling companion, and a young nobleman from Hungary, I now travelled on with a vetturino for five days: solitary, and more picturesque than habitable inns among the Apennines were our night's quarters. At length the Campagna, with its thought-awakening desolation, lay before us.

It was the 31st of March, 1846, when I again saw Rome, and for the third time in my life should reach this city of the world. I felt so happy, so penetrated with thankfulness and joy; how much more God had given me than a thousand others—nay, than to many thousands! And even in this very feeling there is a blessing—where joy is very great, as in the deepest grief, there is only God on whom one can lean! The first impression was—I can find no other word for it—adoration. When day unrolled for me my beloved Rome, I felt what I cannot express more briefly or better that I did

in a letter to a friend : " I am growing here into
the very ruins, I live with the petrified gods, and
the roses are always blooming, and the church
bells ringing—and yet Rome is not the Rome
it was thirteen years ago when I was first here. It
is as if every thing were modernized, the ruins
even, grass and bushes are cleared away. Every
thing is made so neat ; the very life of the people
seems to have retired ; I no longer hear the tam-
bourines in the streets, no longer see the young
girls dancing their Saltarella, even in the Campagna
intelligence has entered by invisible railroads ;
the peasant no longer believes as he used to do.
At the Easter festival I saw great numbers of the
people from the Campagna standing before St.
Peter's whilst the Pope distributed his blessing,
just as though they had been Protestant strangers.
This was repulsive to my feelings, I felt an impulse
to kneel before the invisible saint. When I was
here thirteen years ago, all knelt ; now reason
had conquered faith. Ten years later, when the
railways will have brought cities still nearer to
each other, Rome will be yet more changed. But
in all that happens, every thing is for the best ;
one always must love Rome ; it is like a story

book, one is always discovering new wonders, and one lives in imagination and reality."

The first time I travelled to Italy I had no eyes for sculpture ; in Paris the rich pictures drew me away from the statues ; for the first time when I came to Florence and stood before the Venus de Medicis, I felt as Thorwaldsen expressed, " the snow melted away from my eyes ; " and a new world of art rose before me. And now at my third sojourn in Rome, after repeated wanderings through the Vatican, I prize the statues far higher than the paintings. But at what other places as at Rome, and to some degree in Naples, does this art step forth so grandly into life ! One is carried away by it, one learns to admire nature in the work of art, the beauty of form becomes spiritual.

Among the many clever and beautiful things which I saw exhibited in the studios of the young artists, two pieces of sculpture were what most deeply impressed themselves on my memory ; and these were in the studio of my countryman Jerichau. I saw his group of Hercules, and Hebe which had been spoken of with such enthusiasm in the Allgemeine Zeitung and other German papers, and which, through its antique repose, and its glorious beauty, powerfully seized upon me. My imagination was filled by it, and yet I must place Jerichau's later group, the Fighting Hunter, still higher. It is formed after the model, as though it had sprung from nature. There lies in it truth, a beauty, and a grandeur which I am convinced will make his name resound through many lands !

I have known him from the time when he was almost a boy. We were both of us born on the same island : he is from the little town of Assens. We met in Copenhagen. No one, not even he himself, knew what lay within him ; and half in jest, half in earnest, he spoke of the combat with himself whether he should go to America and become a savage, or to Rome and become a artist— painter or sculptor : that he did not yet know. His pencil was meanwhile thrown away : he modelled in clay, and my bust was the first which he made. He received no travelling stipendium from the Academy. As far as I know, it was a noble-minded woman, an artist herself, unprovided with means, who, from the interest she felt for the spark of genius she observed in him, assisted

him so far that he reached Italy by means of a
trading vessel. In the beginning he worked in
Thorwaldsen's atelier. During a journey of several
years, he has doubtless experienced the struggles
of genius and the galling fetters of want ; but now
the star of fortune shines upon him. When I
came to Rome, I found him physically suffering
and melancholy. He was unable to bear the warm
summers of Italy ; and many people said he could
not recover unless he visited the north, breathed
the cooler air, and took sea-baths. His praises
resounded through the papers, glorious works
stood in his atelier : but man does not live on
heavenly bread alone. There came one day a
Russian Prince, I believe, and he gave a commission
for the Hunter. Two other commissions followed
on the same day. Jerichau came full of rejoicing
and told this to me. A few days after he travelled
with his wife, a highly gifted painter, to Denmark,
from whence, strengthened body and soul, he
returned, with the winter, to Rome, where the
strokes of his chisel will resound, so that, I
hope, the world will hear them. My heart will
beat joyfully with them !

I also met in Rome, Kolberg, another Danish

sculptor, until now only known in Denmark, but there very highly thought of, a scholar of Thorwaldsen's and a favourite of the great master. He honoured me by making my bust. I also sat once more with the kindly Küchler, and saw the forms fresh as nature spread themselves over the canvas.

I sat once again with the Roman people in the amusing puppet theatre, and heard the children's merriment. Among the German artists, as well as among the Swedes and my own countrymen, I met with a hearty reception. My birth-day was joyfully celebrated. Frau von Goethe, who was in Rome, and who chanced to be living in the very house where I brought my Improvisatore into the world, and made him spend his first years of childhood, sent me from thence a large, true Roman bouquet, a fragrant mosaic. The Swedish painter, Södermark, proposed my health to the company whom the Danes, Swedes, and Norwegians had invited me to meet. From my friends I received some pretty pictures and friendly keepsakes.

The Hanoverian minister, Kästner, to whose friendship I am indebted for many pleasant hours, is an extremely agreeable man, possessed of no small talent for poetry, music, and painting. At his house I really saw for the first time flower-painting elevated by a poetical idea. In one of his rooms he has introduced an arabesque of flowers which presents us with the flora of the whole year. It commences with the first spring flowers, the crocus, the snowdrop, and so on; then come the summer flowers, then the autumn, and at length the garland ends with the red berries and yellow-brown leaves of December.

Constantly in motion, always striving to employ every moment and to see everything, I felt, myself at last very much affected by the unceasing sirocco. The Roman air did not agree with me, and I hastened, therefore, as soon as I had seen, the illumination of the dome and the *girandola*, immediately after the Easter festival, through Terracina to Naples. Count Paar travelled with me. We entered St. Lucia: the sea lay before us: Vesuvius blazed. Those were glorious evenings! moonlight nights! It was as if the heavens had elevated themselves above and the stars were withdrawn. What effect of light! In the north the moon scatters silver over the water; here it was gold. The circulating lanterns of the lighthouse now exhibited their dazzling light, now were totally extinguished. The torches of the fishing-boats threw their obelisk-formed blaze along the surface of the water, or else the boat concealed them like a black shadow, below which the surface of the water was illuminated. One fancied one could see to the bottom, where fishes and plants were in motion. Along the street itself thousands of lights were burning in the shops of the dealers in fruit and fish. Now came a troop of children with lights, and went in procession to the church of St. Lucia. Many fell down with their lights ; but above the whole stood, like the hero of this great drama of light, Vesuvius with his blood-red flame and his illumined cloud of smoke.

I visited the islands of Capri and Ischia once more ; and, as the heat of the sun and the strong sirocco made a longer residence in Naples oppressive to me, I went to Sarrento, Tasso's city, where the foliage of the vine cast a shade, and where the air appears to me lighter. Here I wrote these pages. In Rome, by the bay of Naples and amid the Pyrenees, I put on paper the story of my life.

The well-known festival of the Madonna dell'

Arco called me again to Naples, where I took up my quarters at an hotel in the middle of the city, near the Toledo Street, and found an excellent host and hostess. I had already resided here, but only in the winter. I had now to see Naples in its summer heat and with all its wild tumult, but in what degree I had never imagined. The sun shone down with its burning heat into the narrow streets, in at the balcony door. It was necessary to shut up every place; not a breath of air stirred. Every little corner, every spot in the street on which a shadow fell was crowded with working handicraftsmen, who chattered loudly and merrily; the carriages rolled past; the drivers screamed; the tumult of the people roared like a sea in the other streets; the church bells sounded every minute; my opposite neighbour, God knows who he was, played the musical scale from morning till evening. It was enough to make one lose one's senses!

The sirocco blew its boiling-hot breath and I was perfectly overcome. There was not another room to be had at St. Lucia, and the sea-bathing seemed rather to weaken than to invigorate me. I went therefore again into the country; but the sun burned there with the same beams ; yet still the air there was more elastic, yet for all that it was to me like the poisoned mantle of Hercules, which, as it were, drew out of me strength and spirit. I, who had fancied that I must be precisely a child of the sun, so firmly did my heart always cling to the south, was forced to acknowledge that the snow of the north was in my body, that the snow melted, and that I was more and more miserable.

Most strangers felt as I myself did in this, as the Neapolitans themselves said, unusually hot summer ; the greater number went away. I also would have done the same, but I was obliged to wait several days for a letter of credit ; it had arrived at the right time, but lay forgotten in the hands of my banker. Yet there was a deal for me to see in Naples ; many houses were open to me. I tried whether the will were not stronger than the Neapolitan heat, but I fell into such a nervous state in consequence, that till the time of my departure I was obliged to lie quietly in my hot room, where the night brought no coolness. From the morning twilight till midnight roared the noise of bells, the cry of the people, the trampling of horses on the stone pavement, and the before-mentioned practiser of the scale—it was like being on the rack ; and this caused me to give up my journey to Spain, especially as I was assured, for my consolation, that I should find it just as warm there as here. The physician said that, at this season of the year, I could not sustain the journey.

I took a berth in the steamboat Castor for Marseilles ; the vessel was full to overflowing with passengers ; the whole quarter-deck, even the best place, was occupied by travelling carriages ; under one of these I had my bed laid ; many people followed my example, and the quarter-deck was soon covered with mattresses and carpets. It blew strongly ; the wind increased, and in the second and third night raged to a perfect storm ; the ship rolled from side to side like a cask in the open sea ; the waves dashed on the ship's side and lifted up their broad heads above the bulwarks as if they would look in upon us. It was as if the carriages under which we lay would crush us to pieces, or else would be washed away by the sea. There was a lamentation, but I lay quiet, looked up at the driving clouds, and thought upon God and my beloved.

When at length we reached Genoa most of the passengers went on land : I should have been willing enough to have followed their example, that I might go by Milan to Switzerland, but my letter of credit was drawn upon Marseilles and some Spanish sea-ports. I was obliged to go again on board. The sea was calm ; the air fresh ; it was the most glorious voyage along the charming Sardinian coast. Full of strength and new life I arrived at Marseilles, and, as I here breathed more easily, my longing to see Spain was again renewed. I had laid the plan of seeing this country last, as the bouquet of my journey. In the suffering state in which I had been I was obliged to give it up, but I was now better. I regarded it therefore as a pointing of the finger of heaven that I should be compelled to go to Marseilles, and determined to venture upon the journey. The steam-vessel to Barcelona had, in the meantime, just sailed, and several days must pass before another set out. I determined therefore to travel by short days' journeys through the south of France across the Pyrenees.

Before leaving Marseilles, chance favoured me with a short meeting with one of my friends

from the north, and this was Ole Bull ! He came
from America, and was received in France with
jubilees and serenades, of which I was myself a
witness. At the *table d'hote* in the *Hotel des
Empereurs*, where we both lodged, we flew towards
each other. He told me what I should have expected least of all, that my works had also many
friends in America, that people had inquired from
him about me with the greatest interest, and that
the English translations of my romances had been
reprinted, and spread through the whole country
in cheap editions. My name flown over the great
ocean ! I felt myself at this thought quite insignificant, but yet glad and happy ; wherefore
should I, in preference to so many thousand others,
receive such happiness ? I had and still have a
feeling as though I were a poor peasant lad over
whom a royal mantle is thrown. Yet I was and
am made happy by all this ! Is *this* vanity, or
does it show itself in these expressions of my joy ?

Ole Bull went to Algiers, I towards the Pyrenees.
Through Provence, which looked to me quite
Danish, I reached Nimes, where the grandeur
of the splendid Roman amphitheatre at once
carried me back to Italy. The memorials of

antiquity in the south of France I have never
heard praised as their greatness and number
deserve ; the so-called *Maison Quarrée* is still
standing in all its splendour, like the Theseus
Temple at Athens : Rome has nothing so well
preserved.

In Nimes dwells the baker Reboul, who writes
the most charming poems ; whoever may not
chance to know him from those, is however, well
acquainted with him through Lamartine's Journey
to the East. I found him at the house, stepped
into the bakehouse, and addressed myself to a man
in shirt sleeves who was putting bread into the
oven ; it was Reboul himself ! A noble countenance which expressed a manly character greeted
me.   When I mentioned my name, he was
courteous enough to say he was acquainted with
it through the Revue de Paris, and begged me to
visit him in the afternoon, when he should be able
to entertain me better. When I came again I
found him in a little room which might be called
almost elegant, adorned with pictures, casts and
books, not alone French literature, but translations of the Greek classics. A picture on the
wall represented his most celebrated poem, " The

Dying Child," from Marmier's *Chansons du Nord*.
He knew I had treated the same subject, and I
told him that this was written in my school days.
If in the morning I had found him the industrious
baker, he was now the poet completely ; he spoke
with animation of the literature of his country,
and expressed a wish to see the north, the scenery
and intellectual life of which seemed to interest
him. With great respect I took leave of a man
whom the Muses have not meanly endowed, and
who yet has good sense enough, spite of all the
homage paid him, to remain steadfast to his honest
business, and prefer being the most remarkable
baker of Nimes to losing himself in Paris, after a
short triumph, among hundreds of other poets.

By railway I now travelled by way of Mont-
pellier to Cette, with that rapidity which a train
possesses in France ; you fly there as though for
a wager with the wild huntsman. I involuntarily
remembered that at Basle, at the corner of a
street, where formerly the celebrated Dance of
Death was painted, there is written up in large
letters "Dance of Death," and on the opposite
corner "Way to the Railroad." This singular
juxtaposition just at the frontiers of France, gives

play to the fancy ; in this rushing flight it came
into my thoughts ; it seemed as though the steam
whistle gave the signal to the dance. On German
railways one does not have such wild fancies.

The islander loves the sea as the mountaineer
loves his mountains ! Every sea-port town,
however small it may be, receives in my eyes a
peculiar charm from the sea. Was it the sea,
in connexion perhaps with the Danish tongue,
which sounded in my ears in two houses in Cette,
that made this town so homelike to me ? I know
not, but I felt more in Denmark than in the south
of France. When far from your country you
enter a house where all, from the master and
mistress to the servants, speak your own language,
as was here the case, these home tones have a real
power of enchantment : like the mantle of Faust,
in a moment they transport you, house and all, into
your own land. Here, however, there was no
northern summer, but the hot sun of Naples ; it
might even have burnt Faust's cap. The sun's
rays destroyed all strength. For many years there
had not been such a summer, even here ; and from
the country round about arrived accounts of
people who had died from the heat : the very nights

were hot. I was told beforehand I should be unable to bear the journey in Spain. I felt this myself, but then Spain was to be the bouquet of my journey. I already saw the Pyrenees; the blue mountains enticed me—and one morning early I found myself on the steam-boat.

The sun rose higher; it burnt above, it burnt from the expanse of waters, myriads of jelly-like medusas filled the river; it was as though the sun's rays had changed the whole sea into a heaving world of animal life; I had never before seen anything like it. In the Languedoc canal we had all to get into a large boat which had been constructed more for goods than for passengers. The deck was covered with boxes and trunks, and these again occupied by people who sought shade under umbrellas. It was impossible to move; no railing surrounded this pile of boxes and people, which was drawn along by three or four horses attached by long ropes. Beneath in the cabins it was as crowded; people sat close to each other, like flies in a cup of sugar. A lady who had fainted from the heat and tobacco smoke, was carried in and laid upon the only unoccupied spot on the floor; she was brought here for air, but here there was none, spite of the number of fans in motion ; there were no refreshments to be had, not even a drink of water, except the warm, yellow water which the canal afforded. Over the cabin windows hung booted legs, which at the same time that they deprived the cabin of light, seemed to give a substance to the oppressive air. Shut up in this place one had also the torment of being forced to listen to a man who was always trying to say something witty ; the stream of words played about his lips as the canal water about the boat. I made myself a way through boxes, people, and umbrellas, and stood in a boiling hot air ; on either side the prospect was eternally the same, green grass, a green tree, flood-gates—green grass, a green tree, flood-gates—and then again the same ; it was enough to drive one insane.

At the distance of a half-hour's journey from Beziers we were put on land ; I felt almost ready to faint, and there was no carriage here, for the omnibus had not expected us so early ; the sun burnt infernally. People say the south of France is a portion of Paradise ; under the present circumstances it seemed to me a portion of hell with all its heat. In Beziers the diligence was waiting, but all the best places were already taken ; and I here for the first, and I hope for the last time, got into the hinder part of such a conveyance. An ugly woman in slippers, and with a head-dress a yard high, which she hung up, took her seat beside me ; and now came a singing sailor who had certainly drunk too many healths ; then a couple of dirty fellows, whose first manœuvre was to pull off their boots and coats and sit upon them, hot and dirty, whilst the thick clouds of dust whirled into the vehicle, and the sun burnt and blinded me. It was impossible to endure this farther than Narbonne ; sick and suffering, I sought rest, but then came gendarmes and demanded my passport, and then just as night began, a fire must needs break out in the neighbouring village; the fire alarm resounded, the fire-engines rolled along, it was just as though all manner of tormenting spirits were let loose. From here as far as the Pyrenees there followed repeated demands for your passport, so wearisome that you know nothing like it even in Italy : they gave you as a reason, the nearness to the Spanish frontiers, the number of fugitives from thence, and several murders which had taken place in the neighbourhood : all conduced to make the journey in my then state of health a real torment.

I reached Perpignan. The sun had here also swept the streets of people, it was only when night came that they came forth, but then it was like a roaring stream, as though a real tumult were about to destroy the town. The human crowd moved in waves beneath my windows, a loud shout resounded ; it pierced through my sick frame. What was that ?—what did it mean ? " " Good evening, Mr. Arago ! " resounded from the strongest voices, thousands repeated it, and music sounded ; it was the celebrated Arago, who was staying in the room next to mine : the people gave him a serenade. Now this was the third I had witnessed on my journey. Arago addressed them from the balcony, the shouts of the people filled the streets. There are few evenings in my life when I have felt so ill as on this one, the tumult went through my nerves ; the beautiful singing which followed could not refresh me. Ill as I was, I gave up every thought of travelling into Spain ; I felt it would be impossible for me. Ah, if I could only recover strength enough to reach Switzerland ! I was filled with horror at the idea of the journey back. I was advised to hasten as quickly as possible to the Pyrenees, and there breathe the strengthening mountain air : the baths of Vernet were recommended as cool and excellent, and I had a letter of introduction to the head of the establishment there. After an exhausting journey of a night and some hours in the morning, I have reached this place, from whence I sent these last sheets. The air is so cool, so strengthening, such as I have not breathed for months. A few days here have entirely restored me, my pen flies again over the paper, and my thoughts towards that wonderful Spain. I stand like Moses and see the land before me, yet may not tread upon it. But if God so wills it, I will at some future time in the winter fly from the north hither into this rich beautiful land, from which the sun with his sword of flame now holds me back.

Vernet as yet is not one of the well-known bathing places, although it possesses the peculiarity of being visited all the year round. The most celebrated visitor last winter was Ibrahim Pacha ; his name still lives on the lips of the hostess and waiter as the greatest glory of the establishment ; his rooms were shown first as a curiosity. Among the anecdotes current about him is the story of his two French words, *merci* and *très bien*, which he pronounced in a perfectly wrong manner.

In every respect, Vernet among baths is as yet in a state of innocence ; it is only in point of great bills that the Commandant has been able to raise it on a level with the first in Europe. As for the rest, you live here in a solitude, and separated from the world as in no other bathing place : for the amusement of the guests nothing in the least has been done ; this must be sought in wanderings on foot or on donkey-back among the mountains ; but here all is so peculiar and full of variety, that the want of artificial pleasures is the less felt.

It is here as though the most opposite natural productions had been mingled together,—northern and southern, mountain and valley vegetation. From one point you will look over vineyards, and up to a mountain which appears a sample card of corn fields and green meadows, where the hay stands in cocks ; from another you will only see the naked, metallic rocks with strange crags jutting forth from them, long and narrow as though they were broken statues or pillars ; now you walk under poplar trees, through small meadows, where the balm-mint grows, as thoroughly Danish a production as though it were cut out of Zealand; now you stand under shelter of the rock, where cypresses and figs spring forth among vine leaves, and see a piece of Italy. But the soul of the whole, the pulses which beat audibly in millions through the mountain chain, are the springs. There is a life, a babbling in the ever-rushing waters! It springs forth everywhere, murmurs in the moss, rushes over the great stones. There is a movement, a life which it is impossible for words to give; you hear a constant rushing chorus of a million strings; above and below you, and all around, you hear the babbling of the river nymphs.

High on the cliff, at the edge of a steep precipice, lie the remains of a Moorish castle the clouds hang where hung the balcony; the path along which the ass now goes, leads through the hall. From here you can enjoy the view over the whole valley, which, long and narrow, seems like a river of trees, which winds among the red scorched rocks; and in the middle of this green valley rises terrace-like on a hill, the little town of Vernet, which only wants minarets to look like a Bulgarian town. A miserable church with two long holes as windows, and close to it a ruined tower, form the upper portion, then come the dark brown roofs, and the dirty grey houses with opened shutters instead of windows—but picturesque it certainly is.

But if you enter the town itself—where the apothecary's shop is, is also the bookseller's—poverty is the only impression. Almost all the houses are built of unhewn stones, piled one upon another, and two or three gloomy holes form door and windows through which the swallows fly out and in. Wherever I entered, I saw through the worn floor of the first story down into a chaotic gloom beneath. On the wall hangs generally a bit of fat meat with the hairy skin attached; it was explained to me that this was used to rub their shoes with. The sleeping-room is painted in the most glaring manner with saints, angels, garlands, and crowns *al fresco*, as if done when the art of painting was in its greatest state of imperfection.

The people are unusually ugly; the very children are real gnomes; the expression of childhood does not soften the clumsy features. But a few hours journey on the other side of the mountains, on the Spanish side, there blooms beauty, there flash merry brown eyes. The only poetical picture I retain of Vernet was this. In the market-place, under a splendidly large tree, a wandering pedlar had spread out all his wares,—handkerchiefs, books and pictures,—a whole bazaar, but the earth was his table ; all the ugly children of the town, burnt through by the sun, stood assembled round these splendid things ; several old women looked out from their open shops ; on horses and asses the visitors to the bath, ladies and gentlemen rode by in long procession, whilst two little children, half hid behind a heap of planks, played at being cocks, and shouted all the time, "Kekkeriki!"

Far more of a town, habitable and well-appointed, is the garrison town of Villefranche, with its castle of the age of Louis XIV., which lies a few hours' journey from this place. The road by Olette to Spain passes through it, and there is also some business ; many houses attract your eye by their beautiful Moorish windows carved in marble. The church is built half in the Moorish style, the altars are such as are seen in Spanish churches, and the Virgin stands there with the Child, all dressed in gold and silver. I visited Villefranche one of the first days of my sojourn here ; all the visitors made the excursion with me, to which end all the horses and asses far and near were brought together ; horses were put into the Commandant's venerable coach, and it was occupied by people within and without, just as though it had been a French public vehicle. A most amiable Holsteiner, the best rider of the company, the well-known painter Dauzats, a friend of Alexander Dumas', led the train. The forts, the barracks, and the caves were seen ; the little town of Cornelia also, with its interesting church, was not passed over. Everywhere were found traces of the power and art of the Moors ; every thing in this neighbourhood speaks more of Spain than France, the very language wavers between the two.

And here in this fresh mountain nature, on the frontiers of a land whose beauty and defects I am not yet to become acquainted with, I will close these pages, which will make in my life a frontier to coming years, with their beauty and defects. Before I leave the Pyrenees these written pages will fly to Germany, a great section of my life ; I myself shall follow, and a new and unknown section will begin.—What may it unfold ?—I know not, but thankfully, hopefully, I look forward. My whole life, the bright as well as the gloomy days, led to the best. It is like a voyage to some known point.—-I stand at the rudder, I have chosen my path,—but God rules the storm and the sea. He may direct it otherwise; and then, happen what may, it will be the best for me. This faith is firmly planted in my breast, and makes me happy.

The story of my life up to the present hour, lies unrolled before me, so rich and beautiful that I could not have invented it. I feel that I am a child of good fortune; almost every one meets me full of love and candour, and seldom has my confidence in human nature been deceived. From the prince to the poorest peasant I have felt the noble human heart beat. It is a joy to live and to believe in God and man. Openly and full of confidence, as if I sat among dear friends, I have here related the story of my life, have spoken both of my sorrows and joys, and have expressed my pleasure at each mark of applause and recognition, as I believe I might even express it before God himself. But then, whether this may be vanity? I know not: my heart was affected and humble at the same time, my thought was gratitude to God.

That I have related it is not alone because such a biographical sketch as this was desired from me for the collected edition of my works, but because, as has been already said, the history of my life will be the best commentary to all my works.

In a few days I shall say farewell to the Pyrenees, and return through Switzerland to dear, kind Germany, where so much joy has flowed into my life, where I possess so many sympathising friends, where my writings have been so kindly and encouragingly received, and where also these sheets will be gently criticised.

When the Christmas-tree is lighted,—when, as people say, the white bees swarm,—I shall be, God willing, again in Denmark with my dear ones, my heart filled with the flowers of travel, and strengthened both in body and mind : then will new works grow upon paper ; may God lay his blessing upon them ! He will do so. A star of good fortune shines upon me ; there are thousands who deserve it far more than I ; I often myself cannot concieve why I, in preference to numberless others, should receive so much joy : may it continue to shine ! But should it set, perhaps whilst I conclude these lines, still it has shone, I have received my rich portion ; let it set ! From this also the best will spring. To God and men my thanks, my love !

H. C. ANDERSEN.